# *ESPRESSO*

## From Bean to Cup

Nick Jurich

MISSING LINK PRESS, INC., SEATTLE

*from Ming - Christmas '93*

Many of the designations used by manufacturers and sellers to distinguish their products are claimed as trademarks. Where those designations appear and Missing Link Press was aware of a trademark claim, the designations have been printed in initial capital letters.

ISBN 1-880289-00-8

# ACKNOWLEDGEMENTS

My deepest thanks to all my friends from around the country and the world who have contributed so much to the making of this book. Rather than trying to thank them all, I would like to use this space in a manner in which they would all approve.

Many of the richest coffees are grown in some of the world's poorest regions. The organizations listed below have programs aimed at improving the quality of life for the children and families living in those regions.

To give back some of the joy that has been given to us, write or call:

COFFEE KIDS
207 Wickenden Street
Providence, RI 02903
(401) 331-9099

C.A.R.E.
1402 Third Avenue
Suite 912
Seattle, WA 98101
(206) 464-0787

*Dedicated to my family and friends who had the patience and understanding to help make this book possible.*

# CONTENTS

# INTRODUCTION

What is espresso? Espresso is the delicious, romantic beverage brewed only one or two cups at a time, produced as a result of precisely heated water being forced quickly under pressure through carefully ground and packed coffee. The machine used for the process is called an espresso machine. Although espresso can be made with any coffee, classic espresso is most often made with blends of complementary beans that have been dark-roasted to what is often called an espresso roast. The beans are ground to a fine, gritty but not powdery texture that is called an espresso grind. If you have noticed a pattern developing here, you are right. Espresso is a number of different things.

Espresso, when prepared well, is a beverage unsurpassed in its ability to bring out the best in a coffee bean. Pressure coupled with precisely heated water extracts the oils and colloids that are responsible for the body, flavor and aroma of espresso. The extracted colloids lower the surface tension of the espresso, allowing it to penetrate deeper into the taste buds. In simpler terms, the espresso process creates a brew with an intensity of flavor not found in coffee prepared by any other brewing method. Made poorly, espresso becomes a horribly bitter and distasteful brew. When made properly espresso and its variations offer something to satisfy everyone from the daily coffee drinker to those who have always believed they never liked coffee, let alone espresso.

The purpose of this book is to help you prepare perfect espresso consistently and to communicate an understanding, from bean to cup. Your enjoyment will be enhanced by a better understanding of all the elements necessary for great espresso, beginning with the coffee bean itself.

# A History of Coffee

*One of the most interesting facts in the history of coffee
drinks is that wherever it has been introduced it has
spelled revolution. It has been the world's most radical
drink in that its function has always been to make people
think. And when the people began to think, they became
dangerous to tyrants and to foes of liberty of thoughts
and action.*

- William Ukers
*All About Coffee*

AMERICA'S LOVE AFFAIR WITH COFFEE BEGAN OFFICIALLY
at the Boston Tea Party. Shortly afterward, to
protest the British Crown's Tea Tax, the Conti-
nental Congress declared coffee to be the
country's national beverage. The story of coffee would
make an epic film. It is a story of sacrifice, seduction, controversy, political and religious persecution involving
thieves, saboteurs, savage rulers, sleepy monks, songs and
pirouetting goats. A great mixture of fact and fantasy, just
like real life. Now a few excerpts from that colorful history:

Most agree that coffee had been used as a beverage
or food in Ethiopia long before the stories of its "discovery" began circulating.

One of the most popular tales of the bean's discovery concerns a goatherder named Kaldi. One day the
young goatherder noticed that his goats were behaving

strangely. The old buck had lost his dignity and was cavorting about like a young kid. The once goatly demeanor of the rest of the herd had vanished. Kaldi attributed the new attitude of his herd to the berries of a bush that the goats were gleefully eating. Kaldi had recently suffered a lamentable emotional setback. He looked with envy at the cavorting goats and thought, "Why not me?" With dramatic flair, he flung himself upon a bush and gulped berries with abandon. He became the happiest goatherder for miles around. He danced when the goats danced, he ate berries when the goats ate berries and his parents worried. Kaldi could have taken his miraculous discovery to the grave with him, but fate was kind to all of us.

A monk happened by one day and was astounded to see a ball going on. A beautiful ballet was happening in front of him. As the old buck narcissisticly posed, the other goats were pirouetting with remarkable skill and Kaldi danced with wild recklessness. The monk was amazed and asked Kaldi exactly what caused this salubrious madness and Kaldi told him.

Seeing the berries as the solution to his problem of falling asleep during prayers, he believed them to be a gift from God. Godliness doesn't preclude culinary instincts. The monk had the foresight of drying and boiling the fruit of Kaldi. The ingenious monk had given the world coffee. Soon he was the happiest monk for miles around. He and his fellow monks never fell asleep during prayers again. Shortly thereafter, monks everywhere were drinking coffee because it prompted them to pray and because it was not disagreeable.

Though some may question the authenticity of the Kaldi story, everyone seems to agree that coffee began being regularly cultivated in sixth century Yemen, on the Arabian peninsula. Also indisputable is the speed with which the popularity of coffee grew. However, with popularity came trouble.

Although denounced by many religious leaders to be the drink of Satan, people still drank coffee. Coffeehouses were everywhere, and political leaders labelled them as "hotbeds of sedition." The next time you are publicly sipping a cup of coffee, consider the punishment ordered for such an act by the Ottoman Grand Vizier Kuprili. For religious and political reasons, the Grand Vizier had ordered all coffeehouses closed, and cudgeled those who disobeyed the edict. If being severely beaten did not deter the faithful, a second offense resulted in being sewn into a leather bag and thrown into a river. "I'll have an Almond Latte, please." Makes you think twice, doesn't it?

Coffee found its way to Italy and Europe with the help of Venetian trade merchants around 1615. In Italy, the clergy reacted by beseeching Pope Clement VIII to ban the brew since many considered it the drink of the devil. However the Pope, already a coffee drinker, decided to "fool Satan" by baptizing the drink and proclaiming it to be truly a Christian beverage. The Italians' love of coffee grew and strengthened.

Coffeehouses spread rapidly throughout Europe. Their political, social and economical importance should not be overlooked. King Charles II of England outlawed coffeehouses after he noticed that they were attracting both upper and lower classes and that the intellectualizing going on was considerably different than that going on at the pubs. He referred to them as "penny universities." He recanted his decree just eleven days after it was issued as a result of the furor it created. By the end of the 17th Century there were nearly two thousand coffee-houses in London. Lloyd's, a coffee-house frequented by London insurance brokers, was the birthplace of Lloyd's of London. The London

Stock Exchange claims a similar heritage. By 1843 there were more than 3000 coffeehouses in Paris. A Parisian coffeehouse is said to have been the root of the intellectualism that led to the French Revolution.

The Dutch took coffee seeds from Yemen and planted them in their colonies, most notably in Java. One of the most romantic episodes in the history of coffee had to do with a plant that was the property of King Louis XIV of France. Very few Europeans had coffee plants and those who did were looked upon with envy. This particular plant was a treasured gift from the Burgomaster of Amsterdam to the King in 1714. It was coveted by all. The significance of that single plant cannot be overemphasized. Coffee plants are self propagating. The heritage of the majority of the coffee plants alive today in the French Colonies, South and Central America and Mexico can be traced to the coffee plant of King Louis XIV.

It was sometime between 1720 and 1723 that the captain in infantry at Martinique, Captain Gabriel Mathieu de Clieu, arrived at the French colony with the plant or plants he had obtained with great difficulty in France. The plants had finally been successfully procured through a royal physician, M. de Chirac, as a consequence of the charms of a "lady of quality" whom de Chirac was unable to deny.

The journey back to Martinique involved pirates, storms and a calm lengthy enough to warrant the strict rationing of water for the remainder of the trip. Although suffering from thirst, the good Captain shared his daily water ration with the small plant, lovingly caring for it and protecting it from a man who threatened to destroy it due to his jealousy of de Clieu's prize. When the plant finally arrived in Martinique, it was placed under twenty-four-hour guard until it reached maturity. Fifty years later there were nearly nineteen million coffee trees in Martinique.

Coffee plants in Brazil and most of South America are said to be the consequence of an affair involving the wife of the French governor of Guyana and a Brazilian official. A farewell bouquet given to the Brazilian by the woman contained flowering coffee branches.

Coffee has had an effect upon the arts. Johann Sebastian Bach wrote the *Cantata No. 211 (Coffee Cantata)* in 1732, at the height of his creative genius. It is considered among his most perfect works. At the time Bach wrote the Cantata the German public was concerned about the number of women frequenting coffeehouses. In the Cantata, a worried father chastises his daughter for her coffee habit, which she refers to as "my dearest joy." The father implores her to quit, the daughter resists, repeatedly informing him, "Coffee my one only bliss is, sweeter than thousands of kisses, better than sparkling wine." The daughter renounces coffee only when informed she would never find a man willing to marry a woman with a coffee habit.

There is one relatively recent addition to the history of coffee that deserves mention. The Brazilian plantation frosts of 1976 and 1977 caused coffee prices to skyrocket. Prices subsequently declined but never reached their pre-frost levels. Few were willing to pay the price for premium beans before the deadly frosts. However, when faced with considerably higher prices for standard coffee, the cost of the superior beans didn't seem as high. Both the frosts and heightened consumer demand for quality played a part in the subsequent exceptional growth of the specialty coffee market.

The history of coffee is an extraordinary study. If you would like to learn more about it, I heartily recommend the book, *All About Coffee*, by William Ukers. Written in 1928, it is as good a book on coffee as has been written and will delight you with detail.

## *ESPRESSO*

The history of espresso isn't nearly as colorful as that of the bean itself, but that could be due to its youth. Espresso is a relatively modern way of making coffee. The predecessors of modern espresso machines first made their appearance in France in 1822. There is some debate as to who should receive credit for the invention. Most believe that it was either Louis Bernard Rabaut or Michel Varnier.

Edward Loysel de Santais applied the new brewing method to a larger machine in 1843. De Santais' machine

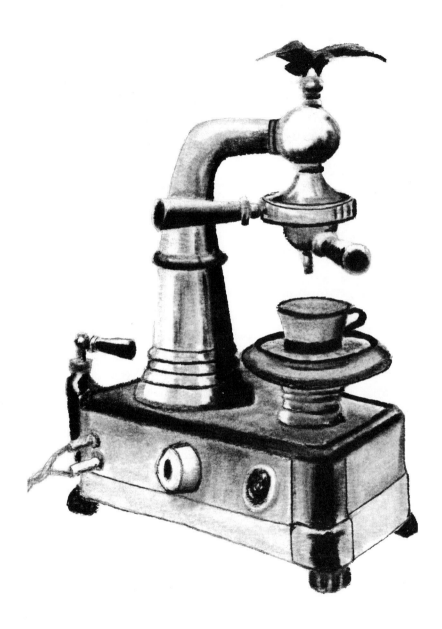

*"La Victoria" Arduino Mignonne*
*One of the early espresso machines, circa 1909*

became the rage of the Paris Exposition of 1855. Capable of brewing 2000 cups an hour, de Santais' machine was still an age away from the machines of today. De Santais' machine used steam pressure rather than utilizing pumps or pistons to force the water through the grounds. His was similar to modern-day mokas and was more likely to produce a pot at a time than an individual cup.

The Italians gave us most of the innovations and refinements that have led to the espresso of today. The first commercially manufactured machines were made by Bezzara of Milan around the turn of the century. The machines evolved into the cafe giants of brass and copper that have contributed so much charm and mystique to espresso over the years. The next development of note came in the thirties, when Francesco Illy used compressed air instead of steam to force the water through the grounds. While affording greater control over temperature, the machines still left a lot to be desired as far as pressure was concerned. These towering marvels with their gleaming boilers, tubes and valves remained the standard commercial machines until World War II.

In 1945, Achille Gaggia gave the world the piston machine. Rather than using steam pressure to force water through the grounds, a piston activated by a lever manipulated by the operator forced the water through the grounds at pressures much higher than those generated by the steam machines.

The first electric pump machines appeared in the early fifties. In the sixties, the spring powered piston gave way to an hydraulic piston. Today, electric pump machines have made the home espresso experience accessible and extraordinarily popular. The history of espresso may be without pirouetting goats, sleepy monks, accommodating ladies of the court, savage tyrants, resourceful Popes or courageous captains, but at least it has produced the perfect way to pay tribute to the remarkable coffee bean.

# The Bean

ANY DO NOT UNDERSTAND THE ECONOMIC IMPACT and importance of coffee. The coffee industry employs over twenty million people worldwide. The United States imports over four billion dollars worth of coffee per year. Coffee is one of the world's most valuable commodities: only oil ranks higher in terms of dollars traded in the international market. Coffee is considerably more romantic than oil – a fact of considerable importance to coffee lovers around the world.

## WHAT YOU GRIND

Coffee grows in the tropics and near tropics from about twenty five degrees north to thirty degrees south of the equator. The two most widely used species of coffee are the *Coffea arabica* (ah-RAH-bee-kah) and the *Coffea robusta* (row-BOOST-ah, or row-BUST-ah). The robusta is a lowland plant much less susceptible to disease than the arabica, being a much hardier plant. Robusta is much less expensive and is considered to be inferior to the arabica. Robusta is the coffee that we grew up with, purchased in cans at the local grocery. The big coffee companies buy robusta to cut costs, blending it with small amounts of arabica for flavor. Robustas have twice the caffeine of arabicas.

Generally, coffees sold in whole bean form are arabicas. The arabica bean is hard and dense and is much more flavorful than the robusta. Arabicas are grown at higher altitudes and grow best between two to six thousand feet, with the finest beans being produced above the four thousand foot level. The greater the altitude, the more slowly the arabicas form, allowing for the development of a more complex and flavorful bean. The arabica plant can grow to a height of eighteen feet. Plants are pruned so they grow no higher than nine feet in order to simplify harvesting. Coffee plants produce their largest crops between the ages of five to thirteen years but remain productive for forty to fifty years. An arabica tree's yearly production equals but one or two pounds of roasted coffee. About five pounds of coffee "cherries" are necessary to produce one pound of roasted coffee. There are approximately three and a half to four thousand beans in a pound of roasted coffee.

## A SEED

A coffee bean is actually the seed of a fruit tree. It is enclosed in a berry that is referred to as a cherry. There are often two beans to a cherry. In the cherry, the beans are covered by several skins and a layer of pulp. The cherries take from six to nine months to develop, and ripen over a period of about three months. In ripening, the cherries turn from green to yellow, then to an orange-red. Cherries on the same tree ripen at different times during the year and are always harvested by hand. Coffee from the same plant can vary from harvest to harvest. No two crops are exactly alike. The coffee plant is affected by changes in climate and soil conditions, as well as harvesting and processing procedures.

# PROCESSING

Processing of the cherries is done in one of two ways. Dry processing is the least expensive and oldest method of removing the husk from the bean. The dry process is often used in areas where water is scarce. The cherries are dried either by the sun or in large mechanical dryers. The dried husks are subsequently removed by either a millstone or a machine. One problem with the dry process is that it can be used on cherries that have not fully ripened. As a result, both overripe and underripe berries can be processed and sold to roasters.

Water process or washed coffees are generally superior. Coffees processed in this manner have the layers of skin and pulp removed from the cherries before they have dried. It is an involved process, one in which the bean, because it is not dry, can be easily damaged. After the layers of skin and pulp have been removed, a last paste-like layer is removed by soaking. Natural enzymes assimilate the last layer in a process called fermentation. When the fermentation process is completed, the beans are washed. When dry, the bean is ready to be bagged and sent to the roasters, where it will be turned into the coffee you purchase.

# GRADING

Among the criteria used for grading coffee beans are species, size, altitude at which grown, color, cup quality, and the process used for gathering and preparation. Although they are standardized in each growing region, grade names differ from one region or country to another. Grading is a relatively straightforward task. Unfortunately, grade names and designations can be vague, confusing, contradictory and illogical. What is more important than learning the various names and designations is a knowledge of the buying standards of the roaster. Ask the simple question, "Do you use the highest available grade of that particular bean?" Good roasters take pride in their art and materials. If they are using a quality bean, they will be more than happy to answer all of your questions.

# BASIC FLAVOR CHARACTERISTICS

Volumes have been written about the flavor characteristics of the coffee bean. Many of the terms are of little importance to the average coffee drinker. What *is* important is for the roaster to understand what is and isn't desirable in a coffee bean. The knowledge of a few basic terms is all that is necessary to better appreciate what we are drinking.

**Flavor** is the most important term, encompassing aroma, acidity and body. Flavor is used to describe the overall impression of the coffee and is also used to individualize characteristics such as "chocolaty" or "spicy." The process used to brew espresso lowers its surface tension. As a result, espresso penetrates more deeply into the taste buds than regularly brewed coffee. Any faults in the beans or roast are amplified and instantly uncovered.

**Aroma** signals the taste of the coffee. Your sense of smell allows you to differentiate between thousands of distinct aromas. Your sense of taste is crude by comparison, capable of distinguishing only four basic sensations. Aroma is your first impression of coffee and is largely responsible for its popularity and allure. Espresso is spectacularly aromatic. Over six hundred different compounds have been identified in the aroma of espresso. No other brewing method is capable of producing an equally mesmerizing aroma. It is an indispensable element in the romance of espresso.

**Acidity** should not be confused with sour, bitter or PH level. Acidity is used to describe the sharp, bright flavor of high-grown coffees and is a pleasing, desirable characteristic.

**Body** is the sensation of consistency, texture and fullness created by the coffee in your mouth. When prepared well, espresso is full-bodied. Unfortunately it can also be watery and thin if not prepared well. The brewing process, the blend and roast, and the skill of the preparer are all responsible for the body of espresso.

**Buttery** is a pleasant term most commonly associated with espresso. It is used to describe the buttery feel created in the mouth by the oils and fats transferred from the beans to the brew. It is included in this abbreviated list for its relation to the fat content of the bean. Fat content is crucial for the formation of the delectable "crema" or froth that contains the aroma of a good espresso.

## UNFORTUNATE ATTRIBUTIONS

**Bitter**, **burnt** and **scorched** are terms that are all too often unfairly associated with espresso. The first two are flavor characteristics most often related to the roasting process. Bitterness is a taste found in dark-roasted coffees and is the most acceptable of the three terms. The darker the roast, the greater the bitterness. Burnt is an undesirable flavor and is self-explanatory. Burnt can be avoided by choosing the right roast. Bitterness as the result of overextraction is unacceptable and is very different than the bitterness caused by the roast. Too little coffee, too fine a grind, or trying to brew too much coffee from the grounds are brewing errors that result in overextraction. Scorched is also a term linked to preparation and is not a fault of the coffee or roast. It is a term most commonly associated with espresso brewed by commercial machines using too high a brewing temperature. Scorching can occur in your home machine as a result of too fine a grind. The taste of the scorched grounds ends up in your cup. The proper grind will be explained later in the book. Espresso should not be bitter, burnt or scorched. The beans, combined with the roast, the quality of the equipment and the skill of the preparer should create a brew that is very smooth and *bittersweet* with a wonderful aftertaste that lingers pleasantly on the palate for twenty to twenty-five minutes. Espresso should taste as good as it smells.

## *BLENDING*

A blend is a combination of two or more straight coffees in proportions meant to enhance and complement the qualities of each. Straight coffees, also referred to as "varietals," are those from one growing region, country or estate. Blending offers roasters the opportunity to explore flavor potential not possible with a single coffee. Roasters try to develop blends that can be duplicated with combinations of other beans. Such blending is a necessity if the roaster wants to keep the flavor of a specific blend alive in spite of the fluctuating availability of some coffees. Blending is usually done after roasting to best accentuate the highlights of each coffee. Dark roasts are primarily blends. Most roasters will limit their dark roasting to blends or a small variety of coffees. The distinctive taste of dark-roasted coffee can partially or completely overpower the individual characteristics of some coffees.

## *ESPRESSO BLENDS*

The blend is an integral part of the espresso process. Blends and blending procedures have existed for generations in many roasting families and companies. The variety developed as a result of cultural and competitive pride is a source of joy to espresso lovers everywhere. Many roasters believe blends are necessary because no single coffee can provide all the elements essential for great espresso. The most important element of a blend is the quality of the beans. Poor quality beans cannot be hidden in a blend. Many roasters have had longstanding success in the espresso business. Their commitment to quality is the basis of their longevity. They use only the best beans available.

As a romantic, I reluctantly admit that in addition to being an art, espresso is also a science. Coffees are chosen for the particular characteristics they can offer the blend. They are selected for body, aroma, flavor, acidity, fat content, balance, and overall bean quality. Each trait and attribute is important. Selected coffees must complement and interact well with one another in order to achieve the correct balance necessary for a great espresso. No two coffee crops are the same, making blending an art that depends upon the ability of the roaster to adapt to an ever-changing palette.

## *ROASTING*

Roasting itself is also a combination of art and science. Even the best blends and straight coffees would be disappointing without the proper roast. It is the most important step in the coffee's passage from flower to cup. Only through roasting can the delicate coffee oil or coffee essence, be formed. Sugars, starches and fats caramelize and are transformed into the fragile coffee oil as a result of the roasting process. "Oil" really is a misnomer for the substance that gives coffee its flavor and aroma and the dark roasts their characteristic sheen. If the oil was not water soluble, coffee would not be nearly as delicious as it is.

The more than six hundred compounds responsible for the flavor and aroma of coffee are developed during the roasting process. Their formation as well as that of the coffee oil is dependent upon the skill of the roaster. Roast time is critical to the proper development of the coffee oil and determines what qualities of the coffee will develop. If not roasted long enough, the fats and carbohydrates will not have completely caramelized and the coffee oil will not have sufficiently developed. The resulting coffee will be weak, watery and sour. The cinnamon roast is lightest of the roasts. The coffee in cans at the grocery are most commonly roasted to a cinnamon roast.

There is no such thing as a roast that is universally applicable to all varieties of coffee. Coffee beans differ as much as grapes do that are used to make wine. A roast that successfully develops the potential of one coffee may be completely wrong for another. A number of different flavor effects can be attained with the same beans by varying the length of time the beans are roasted. Most specialty coffee roasters will roast their straight and blended coffees to the middle roasts. City and Full City are two of the many names often used to identify the varying degrees of the middle roasts, with City being lighter than

Full City. Regional and roaster preference dictate what degree of roast will be chosen.

Dark roasts are those coffees that have been roasted longer than the norm. The longer the roasting process the more the flavors of the particular coffee are blended with a deepening bittersweet tang that distinguishes the dark roasts from others. The amount of of oil drawn to the surface of a bean increases in direct proportion to the length of roasting time. Any roast of coffee can be used to make espresso, but classical espresso is made from the dark roasts. Lighter roasts are not commonly used to make espresso. The result would be a bitter cup of espresso. The espresso process accentuates the acids in coffee and the light roasts contain higher levels of acid than the dark roasts. Dark roasts can range in color from a light chocolate tan to almost black. The darker the color, the more you will taste the flavor created by the roast rather than the flavor of the bean itself. The darkest roasts will have a heavy, smoky flavor better suited for drip coffee than espresso. The coffee oil sheen can be a beautiful satin-like polished luster in the lightest of the dark roasts to a very obvious oily shine in the darkest. If beans are roasted too long, they will burn along with the coffee oil. The resultant bitter, charcoal-like substance is all too often sold as dark roast coffee by those who either do not understand the complexities of the roast or are trying to hide less-than-stellar beans.

## *CHOOSING A ROAST FOR ESPRESSO*

Choosing a roast that is too dark is the most common mistake made when selecting a roast for espresso. It is important to understand that there is a substantial difference in taste between a lighter dark roast and one that is very dark. Some commendable roasters offer a variety of different roasts and blends specifically made for espresso. The flavor notes of the coffee will be more obvious in the lighter of the dark roasts and they should be used if you want espresso without the typical dark roast tang. If new to the world of espresso, start out with the lightest of the dark roasts and proceed from there.

## A MISCONCEPTION ABOUT DARK ROASTS AND ESPRESSO

Dark roasts are often thought to contain higher levels of caffeine and the acidity that cause the nervousness and discomfort experienced by some as a consequence of drinking coffee. In reality, dark-roast coffees have less caffeine and contain significantly less acid than the lighter. Those who buy the commercial coffees in cans at the local supermarket are usually the first to say no to an espresso because "all that caffeine" would keep them up all night. Espresso, however, is made with less coffee per cup than regularly brewed coffee and is created by a process proven to leave more caffeine in the grounds and less in the cup. Couple the reduction in caffeine caused by the extended roasting time with the fact that espresso is made from arabicas that contain only half the caffeine of the robustas and one wonders who is ingesting more caffeine.

## WHAT'S IN A NAME?

Roasts are not standardized. Espresso, Viennese, Italian and French are all roast names and have nothing to do with the type of coffee used in them. They refer to the degree of roasting with Viennese being the lightest, and Espresso, French and Italian typically being the darkest. "Typically," because each roaster has a different opinion as to how each roast should be defined. A Viennese roast can be either a degree of dark roasting or a blend of dark and light-roast coffees, even in the same city. The roasts will vary from roaster to roaster as well as from region to region. What is one roast in Seattle, will be another in Chicago, San Francisco, New York, Atlanta, New Orleans, and so on.

It is confusing, but don't worry. It doesn't matter. What matters more than the name is the skill of the roaster. The best way to determine the degree of roast is to ask the roaster. The next best way is to look at the color and luster of the beans. The darker the color and the greater the amount of oil on the surface of the beans, the greater the degree of roast. Although variables such as the length of time and temperature at which the coffee is roasted can affect the appearance and flavor of the beans, color and luster are consistent roast degree indicators.

## *WHAT'S IN A NAME? – PART TWO*

A trip to the roaster or coffee retailer can be confusing. There are so many coffees with so many different names. Then there are the blends of two or more straight coffees, whose names can be confusing. Fortunately, sorting them out can be simple.

Coffees with names like Harrar, Celebes, Guatemalan Antigua, Costa Rica Tres Rios, Java, Kona, Ethiopian Yergacheffe, and countless others with similarly tropical or exotic names refer to the origin of the bean. This can include the country, region, growing area, or specific plantation on which it was grown or even the port from which the coffee was shipped. Each name identifies a specific coffee. Grade designations frequently follow the name and can create some confusion, but the more specific the name, the more readily identifiable the coffee.

Confusion can occur when the word "style" is added to a name. Coffees with names like "Jamaican Blue Mountain Style", or "Kona Style" are usually blends of lesser quality beans and often do not have any beans of the type that the name implies.

The most confusing coffees are those whose names give no indication of where they are grown or what is in them. They range from the perfectly legitimate, such as "House Blend," to the nonsensical, such as "London Morning Mist," or "Breath of a Jamaican Dog." The names given to some of the mysterious blends can sound as though the roaster was a frustrated romantic novelist before going into the coffee business. Find out what beans were used in the blends. A flowery name can hide a dubious heritage. The great majority of roasters identify what is in their blends, but do not be suspicious of the reluctance of a roaster to divulge the content or proportions of legitimate blends. Many take years to develop and the originators are understandably protective. Espresso blends are perfect examples.

## THE ROASTER AS ARTIST

The style of the roaster is the result of the blend of his skill, training, understanding, experience, dedication and inspiration. Though the roaster may possess the tools to roast coffee, style determines the quality of the finished product. Roaster style is a welcome and essential variable in the world of gourmet coffee. Multiply the different approaches to roasting and blending by the variety of coffee found in the world and you have a formula that guarantees a remarkable range of flavor and enjoyment for the consumer.

# FINDING YOUR FAVORITE

One of the nicest things about coffee is its accessibility. It has some snobbery associated with it, but most often people in the trade are very accommodating. Ask questions if you don't understand what you are buying. There is an endless variety to be found; don't limit yourself by sticking with one roast or type of coffee. If you don't explore all the possibilities, you'll always wonder what you missed.

# Packaging

*I*F YOU ARE UNABLE TO FIND FRESH BULK COFFEE AND don't want to wait for a delivery from the roaster, you have another alternative. Whole bean coffee is available canned or bagged. If you are buying directly from a roaster, coffee is often packaged in plain or lined paper bags and should be transferred to an airtight container as soon as possible. When storing coffee at home an airtight container is a must. However, this isn't necessarily the best way for a roaster to package freshly roasted beans for the trip to the store.

> *It is circumstance and proper timing that give an action its character and make it either good or bad.*
> - Agesilaus

When beans are freshly roasted, they produce carbon dioxide and will for some time. The roasted beans therefore cannot be sealed in a bag or can until the gas has dissipated or is under control. Otherwise bags will burst and cans will begin to resemble footballs. However if the bags aren't sealed, air can enter and allow the beans to go stale. Whole bean coffee continues to produce gas for weeks after roasting. Simply letting the gas dissipate is unacceptable since the beans would be stale before reaching the store.

# THE VACUUM METHOD

*Nature abhors a vacuum.*

- Benedict Spinoza

Years ago, a very strong vacuum was used to offset the gas in whole bean coffee. The vacuum removed much of the carbon dioxide, but in doing so it also pulled aromatics out of the coffee, robbing it of flavor. Gas is not a problem with ground coffee since the majority dissipates as a result of grinding. Ground coffee is already past its prime when vacuum-packed in a can. But if aromatics were removed from cans of ground coffee, why was there such a wonderfully tantalizing aroma when one was opened? That aroma was *injected.* When I discovered the deception, I was more hurt than when I was told the news about Santa Claus. At least with Santa, I had suspected something wasn't exactly right.

## THE ONE-WAY VALVE

The next evolution in packaging marked the beginning of the return of the aromatics: a small valve was placed on the package that allowed gasses to escape, but no air to enter. The valve works using a very simple principle. When the pressure inside the bag exceeds that outside, the valve is pushed open by the pressure of the gasses. When the pressure inside the bag is equal to that outside the bag, the valve closes.

The return of the aromatics was brought about by the reduction and, in many cases, the elimination of the use of the vacuum to remove air from the bag just prior to sealing. How is the air removed if it is not pulled out by a vacuum? The air is pushed out by flushing the package with an inert gas such as carbon dioxide or nitrogen. The air is removed and the beans are happy. The package will soften as the coffee continues to emit gasses and should not be a source of concern as long as the bag is well sealed. Incidentally, giving the package of beans a squeeze to savor the aroma does not harm the coffee and may very well help to expel any remaining oxygen. The beans will retain a superior level of freshness and flavor.

## *SUMMARY*

When buying bagged coffee, remember that a chain is only as strong as its weakest link. If a bag isn't roaster sealed, leave it at the store. Once a bag is opened, the valve is of no use, and you should transfer the beans to an airtight container as soon as possible.

# Buying The Beans

**F**ORTUNATELY FOR COFFEE DRINKERS EVERYWHERE, THE availability of good whole bean coffee has increased dramatically due to increased interest and demand. Unfortunately, just because whole bean coffee is available, it doesn't necessarily follow that it is fresh or of good quality. No matter if you live where there are a number of roasters and retailers, or only one, or none at all, there are things you can do to better your chances of getting fresh coffee beans.

## ROASTERS AND THEIR RETAIL SHOPS

The best place to buy coffee is at the retail shops of the local roaster. Most have a policy of discarding coffees that have not been sold in a specific period of time, assuring you of getting a fresh bean. They are also the best places to learn about coffee and equipment. Coffee is an accessible and affordable luxury, and just about everyone in the business is very helpful. Be sure to ask all the questions you can. If you are not fortunate enough to live in a city that is home to a roaster or to one of their retail shops, you can still have access to a tremendous variety of the world's finest and freshest coffees.

*Neither snow, nor rain, nor heat, nor gloom of night stays these couriers from the swift completion of their appointed rounds.*

- Inscription, New York City Post Office

You are only as far away as the "Sources" section of this book and a telephone. By ordering your coffee through the mail and directly from the roaster (roaster, not distributor), you can get coffee that is often more recently roasted than many you might find at a low volume "gourmet" shop or supermarket. If you think ordering coffee through the mail is too much trouble, you are wrong. It takes only a phone call and the people are helpful and accommodating. If you have a favorite coffee or roast, many will accommodate a standing order, giving you roaster-fresh coffee at your doorstep week after week. Even if you live miles from the nearest town, you are never out of reach of the perfect cup of espresso.

## SPECIALTY SHOPS

Specialty shops buy their coffee from roasters or distributors. As long as they are conscientious about the coffee they sell, specialty shops are good places to buy coffee. The specialty shops offer you the benefit of being able to browse the machines and other helpful items that may catch your eye. If sales volume is slow, beware. You may be better off buying your coffee in a supermarket or by mail.

## SUPERMARKETS

Supermarkets can be a great places to buy good quality fresh coffee. They may also be places to buy stale coffee. It depends on the sales volume, the attitude of the store and the coffee climate of the town. If the supermarket sells a substantial volume of coffee, the chances of getting fresh beans from them should be good. You should also realize a savings over the specialty shops.

## THE BUYING ESSENTIALS

*He was as fresh as the month of May.*
- Geoffrey Chaucer

Coffee must be fresh. Regardless of where you buy your coffee, find out when it was roasted. Ideally, coffee should be roasted no more than ten to a maximum of fourteen days prior to use. Ask the retailer if they have a policy of discarding stock that has not sold during a specified length of time.

*Training is everything. The peach was once a bitter almond; cauliflower is nothing but cabbage with a college education.*
- Mark Twain

Don't pay a premium price for a lesser quality product. Find out where the beans are from as well as the grade of bean used. If they are of a high quality, they should be able to tell you the origin of the beans. The more specific the name of the coffee used the better. "Costa Rica Tres Rios" is more specific and preferable to a coffee described simply as "Central American."

*By the work one knows the workman.*
- Jean de La Fontaine

Ask the retailer if they roast their own coffee. It is ideal if they do, or if they have it done for them by a nearby roaster. If the coffee is sold under the name of the retailer and not that of the roaster, ask them who supplies the coffee and if that supplier is also the roaster. Coffee sold under the name of the specialty shop may be the same coffee sold for less in the local supermarket under the supermarket's name with neither being the roaster. If the specialty shop has a policy of discarding coffee after a certain period of time and the supermarket does not have a similar policy or a sufficient volume of sales to ensure freshness, you would be wise to pay the premium for the coffee at the specialty shop. If neither policy nor volume is found, call a roaster.

Bins are a very appealing way of displaying beans as long as they are shielded from sunlight, other harsh direct light and are routinely cleaned. An oily, shiny bean is no indication of a fresh bean. The surface oils of coffee will spoil over time. If the retailer puts additional beans in a bin that has not been cleaned for some time, the new beans will be tainted by the residue of the old.

# How To Store Coffee

*L*EAVE SOME AT THE STORE. COFFEE BEGINS GOING STALE before you buy it, so purchase small quantities. Buy only as much as you can drink in a short period of time, a week to ten days.

## GROUND RULES

Store only whole bean coffee. As soon as the bean is broken by grinding and the memorable aroma is released, the coffee begins a rapid decline. Flavor begins to become a memory. Aromatics and oils begin evaporating and oxidizing quickly even in whole bean form, let alone when ground. As that fragrance gently drifts past your nose, it is also drifting past your cup. There is a time and place for everything. The best time to grind is just before you brew.

Evaporation and oxidation aren't the only perils facing ground coffee. Once the bean is broken, absorption becomes a problem. The coffee bean is fibrous and is therefore absorbent by nature. There is a very good reason that ground coffee was once recommended as a refrigerator deodorizer. Coffee, both ground and whole, absorbs moisture and odors indiscriminately. If it is in the air, coffee will soak it up.

# A MULTITUDE OF OPINIONS

*We rarely find that people have good sense unless they agree with us.*

- Francois, Duc de La Rochefoucauld

The enemies of coffee are time, air, light, heat and moisture. It's ironic that the last two are also those things that help us enjoy coffee as much as we do.

There is one common thread among the number of different opinions about how and where to store your whole bean coffee. Everyone agrees that coffee should be stored in an airtight container. Unless the bag the coffee came in is airtight, incorporates a one-way valve (a small plastic button designed to let gasses escape, but not allowing them in) and has not been opened, do not use the bag to store your coffee.

The ceramic canisters modelled after French-style canning jars seem to be the most popular and are widely available. The rubber gasket between the lid and jar provides a good airtight seal. They come in a variety of sizes. Most people buy those that are too large. Each time you open the canister, the coffee is exposed to more air. It is inevitable that air and moisture will come in contact with your coffee beans. You can limit that amount of air and moisture by storing your beans in smaller canisters. Though they aren't nearly as stylish as the ceramic or glass jars, small glass or acrylic containers with Tupperware-like lids are perfect for storing coffee. Glass is preferable to plastic. I store my beans in one-half to one cup containers, opening the next only as the last is emptied. If you like a variety of different coffees, the containers are easy to label.

# TO FREEZE OR NOT TO FREEZE

*A few strong instincts, and a few plain rules.*

- William Wordsworth

Controversy abounds on the subject of whether to freeze or refrigerate coffee. Earlier I mentioned that ground coffee can be used as a refrigerator deodorizer. Coffee both in ground and whole bean form is incredibly absorbent, soaking up any moisture or odor that may be present. People complain about things "tasting like the refrigerator." You will not find a coffee bin labelled "Refrigerator Blend" among the flavored coffees at the local supermarket and for good reason. No one likes coffee that tastes and smells like a large kitchen appliance. Don't store coffee in the refrigerator.

Freezing is the method favored by many to prolong the life of their coffee. Freezing has a less damaging effect on light roasts than dark roasts. However, I don't recommend it for either. I'm not aware of many foods that improve once they are frozen. Experts disagree about the effect that freezing has on the fragile coffee oil. Coffee oil is water soluble and will therefore freeze. As a result of the extended roast time for dark roasts, the coffee oil and aromatics are drawn to the surface of the bean. By being on the surface, the flavor of dark-roast coffee is essentially laid bare with nothing to protect it and is exceptionally vulnerable to damage. Once the delicate oils and aromatics are congealed by freezing, they are never the same.

The only time you should freeze coffee is when you have to keep it longer than two weeks. If such a circumstance arises, there are some rules that should be followed. You must keep the coffee in airtight containers. If you do not, freezer burn will result and while a coffee with freezer burn is more savory than one that tastes like the refrigerator, neither is very pleasant. Return the coffee to the freezer as quickly as possible to prevent condensation which will encourage freezer burn. Use smaller containers in order to limit exposure of the beans.

## COOL, DARK, AND DRY

*Nothing is given so profusely as advice.*
- Francois, Duc de La Rochefoucauld

The best place to store coffee is in a cool, dark, and dry place. Heat, sunlight and moisture are to be avoided. Remember: The most skillful brewer using the finest brewing methods cannot produce a quality cup using a stale or damaged bean.

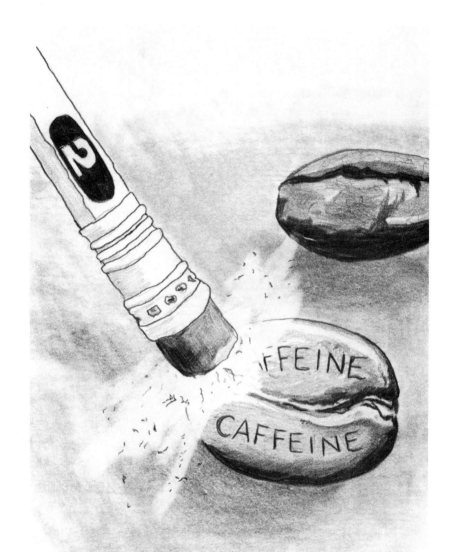

# Decaffeinated Coffee

*I*N ORDER FOR A COFFEE TO BE CONSIDERED DECAF-feinated, 97% of the caffeine existing in the bean must be removed. Caffeine is a naturally occurring chemical in coffee and is a stimulant to the central nervous system.

When people say they don't like decaffeinated coffee because "it doesn't taste like coffee without the caffeine," they are on the right track but it isn't the caffeine that makes the difference. When the taste of "decaf" is sub par, it is usually due to the quality of the bean, the skill (or lack thereof) of the roaster or the process used to decaffeinate, not the lack of caffeine. Since the flavor of a coffee is negatively affected by the decaffeinating process, some roasters will not use their best coffees for their decafs.

As a result of the decaffeination process, the beans become more difficult to roast and are darker than those which have not been decaffeinated. When placed side by side, the decaffeinated coffee should be darker than the same coffee that has not been decaffeinated but has been roasted the same length of time. Keep this fact in mind when you are at the retailer choosing your decaffeinated espresso by the color of the roast.

The first step in decaffeinating is to bathe the bean with a combination of steam and water. Doing so separates but does not remove the caffeine from an acid in the bean, bringing it to the surface. Removal of the caffeine is most often accomplished by one of three methods.

## DIRECT METHOD

The direct method begins by steaming, then soaking the beans in warm water containing a chemical that dissolves the caffeine that has been brought to the surface. The water containing the solvent and caffeine is removed. Fresh water is added to replace the moisture removed from the beans.

The most commonly used solvent is methylene chloride. Unfortunately, the direct method troubles some coffee drinkers. "Unfortunately," for two reasons. First, it has the least effect on coffee flavor of any decaffeinating process. Secondly, methylene chloride vaporizes at 104°F. The final step in the direct contact method is to spray the beans with a jet of steam. Coffee is roasted for about 15 minutes or more at temperatures exceeding 375°F and is then brewed at greater temperatures than the 104°F at which the methylene chloride vaporizes. The occasional few parts per million found in *green* coffee would find the journey to the cup more than a little difficult.

The FDA, as well as a great number of independent testing laboratories and consumer groups, has tested coffees decaffeinated using methylene chloride and found the coffees to be free of the chemical. For an easily accessible test of decaffeinated coffees, go to the library and ask for the September, 1987 issue of *Consumer Reports.*

# WATER PROCESS

This process uses a solvent but in a different manner than previously described. After steaming, the beans are put in a tank containing only water. The caffeine leaches into the water. The water containing the caffeine is transferred to another tank where a solvent is used to remove the caffeine. The same water is then returned to the tank with the beans, allowing the beans to absorb the water minus the caffeine. The solvent never really combines with the water and is therefore more easily removed. Replenishing the bean with the same water allows the bean to absorb flavor that may have leached from it to the water.

# SWISS WATER PROCESS

The Swiss Water Process is the best known of several methods that decaffeinate without the use of chemicals. Caffeine is removed by soaking the beans in hot water for an extended period of time. The caffeine-laden water is then channelled through a series of charcoal filters that remove the caffeine. The decaffeinated water is then returned to the beans. The process does not use any chemicals but removes more of the flavor oils than the previous methods.

# SUMMARY

Choose the decaffeinating method that best suits your own convictions. Coffees decaffeinated by all three methods are widely available and should be easy to locate. More difficult will be finding the talented roaster capable of turning the decaffeinated green coffee bean into one that will make you smile.

# Thoughts About Caffeine

*Tis not the drinking that is to be blamed, but the excess.*

- John Selden

CAFFEINE IS A STIMULANT TO THE CENTRAL NERVOUS system and is found naturally in coffee, tea, cocoa and in over 60 different plants. Caffeine is also found in about 1,000 prescription pharmaceuticals and about 2,000 over-the-counter medications. Taken in moderation, caffeine can increase alertness as well as stimulate thought.

Many people do not realize that caffeine is also added to many colas, some of which having as much caffeine as a cup of arabica coffee. This means that by drinking sodas, many children have a caffeine intake higher than some adults.

Caffeine has long been a source of controversy. Countless studies have been done on the effect of caffeine with the results being vague and contradictory.

Studies have shown that coffee raises blood pressure. Studies have shown that coffee lowers blood pressure. Coffee causes colon cancer. Coffee protects against colon cancer. Coffee increases chances of coronary heart disease and stroke. Coffee has no effect on coronary heart disease and stroke; and so on. The experts are only in agreement that pregnant women should limit their caffeine intake.

An article published in the October 11, 1990 issue of *The New England Journal of Medicine* reported that evidence could not be found to suggest that caffeine or coffee consumption increased the risk of coronary heart disease or stroke. In keeping with the air of confusion and discovery, the study also found that consuming large quantities of decaffeinated coffee might actually cause a mild increase in the risk of cardiovascular disease, but further study was required. The same article also cited problems with much of the research that was done. Often the control groups were too small and other factors such as smoking were not necessarily taken into account.

On the positive side, recent studies have shown that coffee can make senior citizens and those who hope to eventually become senior citizens, "friskier." Also, people suffering from asthma are said to achieve some degree of relief after drinking coffee.

Caffeine should be respected as the stimulant it is and should not be consumed in excess. If you are a lover of coffee, buy only arabica coffee which contains half the caffeine of the more widely available robusta. A cup made from ordinary canned coffee can contain as much as 150mg of caffeine. By comparison, a cup of coffee made from arabicas contains about 70 to 100mg of caffeine. Use a dark roast and you further decrease caffeine intake. Drink espresso or drinks made with espresso since less coffee is used per cup. A cup of espresso can contain as little as 60 to 90mg of caffeine. Drink espresso if you want to limit your caffeine intake but still enjoy a great cup of coffee. As Publius Terentius said over 2,000 years ago, "Moderation in all things."

# Espresso Machines

*T*ODAY'S ESPRESSO MACHINES OFFER AN EASE OF OPERA-
tion that should not intimidate anyone. There are
machines that provide for all levels of ability. The
following will give you a better understanding of
how espresso machines work and will serve as a guide to
help you find the machine that is right for you.

## DETERMINE YOUR NEEDS

Before you spend a good deal of money on an espresso machine, you must decide how serious you are
about espresso. If you like espresso more for the flavor of
the steamed milk in cappuccinos and lattes or for the
chocolate in mochas, with the flavor of the espresso being
of secondary importance, then an inexpensive steam
machine or "moka" and a milk steamer may be for you.
But if you truly care about the taste of espresso and would
like to produce a memorable cup, you will have to invest
in a quality machine. Determine how often you will use
your machine. I use mine daily. I love the versatility that it
offers: I can make a full mug Americano, a demitasse of
espresso, a cappuccino, a mocha, or any other variation
that my taste and imagination will allow. The espresso
method is simple, fresh, without waste, and better than
any other brewing method.

When I want a cup of coffee, I don't need to make a full pot. I don't need to drink a less flavorful cup or throw out the remaining coffee I can't finish. If I, or someone else want another cup, I make another. My espresso machine makes it possible.

## UNDERSTANDING THE ESPRESSO MAKER

Espresso makers can be divided into two categories: stovetop and electric. The stovetop machines work with steam pressure created by an outside heat source.

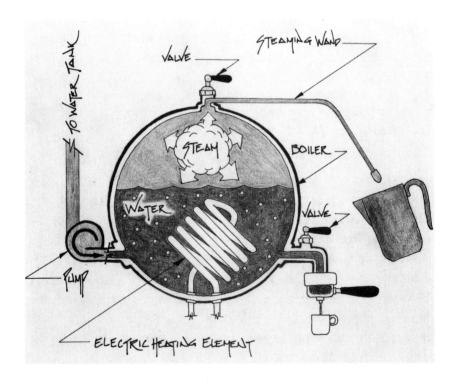

**BASIC OPERATION OF THE ESPRESSO MAKER**

*Water heated in an enclosed chamber is forced through carefully compacted coffee grounds by steam pressure or by a pump or piston. Steam machines operate without a pump or piston and use either an electric heating element or an outside heat source.*

Electric machines create steam internally. Most espresso makers sold today are electric. Although espresso makers vary greatly in performance and the quality of the espresso they produce, their principle of operation is the same: water heated in an enclosed chamber is forced quickly under pressure through compacted coffee grounds.

## MOKAS

Moka is the generic name given to the simplest of the espresso makers. It looks like an old-fashioned stovetop percolator with faceted sides and a belt tightened around its midsection, giving it an angular hourglass look. It is a machine with upper and lower compartments that screw together, holding a strainer filled with the coffee grounds securely between them. Attached to the bottom of the strainer is a hollow shaft that descends to a point just above the floor of the lower compartment. The water in the lower compartment is heated, producing steam. The pressure created by the steam forces the water up the hollow shaft, through the grounds and up another shaft where it dribbles down into the upper compartment of the Moka. The top of the shaft in the upper compartment is fitted with a flow-reducing cap to produce greater pressure in the compartment holding the grounds. Espresso at its simplest. What is produced doesn't resemble the espresso from a good electric machine in appearance or taste. To an Italian, espresso is more than a way to make coffee. Espresso is considered a culture and Mokas are an integral and beloved element of that culture. They are the predecessors of the modern electric espresso machine. Mokas are popular and cheap ($15 and up). Buy Mokas made of stainless steel, since coffee flavor can be tainted by pots made of aluminum.

THE MOKA

*A cornerstone of Italian coffee culture*

The Moka has many shortcomings. Espresso is best when made under more pressure than the Moka is capable of generating. The Moka gives you no control over the pressure, so as soon as enough is generated, the water is sent through the grounds with a force that is far too weak to be effective. Using an external heat source gives only marginal control over temperature, a problem common to all stovetop machines. Although enough pressure to brew can be generated without boiling, boiling can easily occur before the end of the brewing cycle, scalding the coffee and leaving you with a bitter cup. Versatility is also a problem. Mokas can't steam milk, so a separate steamer would be needed if you want to make anything other than plain espresso.

## *STOVETOP ESPRESSO MAKERS*

Greater versatility is offered by the stovetop machines that incorporate a steaming wand and a valve for controlling coffee flow. These machines can make good espresso with more fuss than I care to endure. I have several different stovetop machines that spend their time on the shelf for that very reason.

With these stovetop machines you have a valve that gives you control over flow, but they can make only the number of cups the machine was designed to brew, be it two, three or four. Greater brewing pressure is generated as a result of the control given by the flow valve, giving these machines a definite advantage over the Moka.

The grind used in these machines needs to be precise and leaves little room for error. You will need to use a tamp and grind that will give just the right amount of resistance to the water being forced through the coffee. Too fine a grind coupled with too hard a tamp will make you realize why they put safety valves on espresso makers. Safety is a greater concern with the stovetops than it is with electric machines. Anytime you use an appliance that utilizes an outside heat source, you have to exercise care. One of my concerns with the stovetop machines is their use with the spiral burner elements of electric stoves.

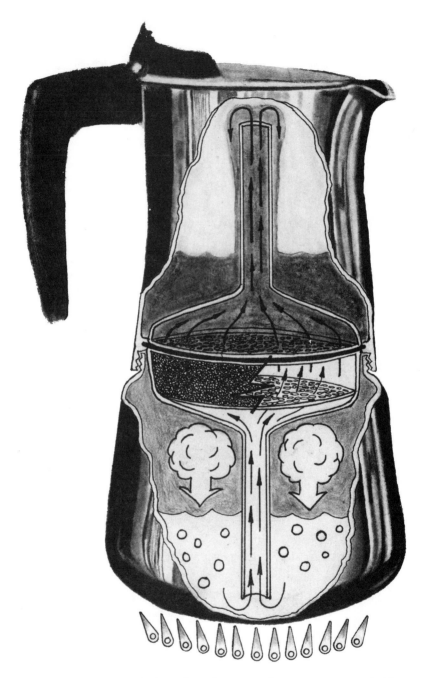

*Coffee grounds provide the only resistance to the pressure generated by steam in Mokas and other stovetop espresso makers that do not use a valve to control water flow.*

Some stovetop machines don't fit well on the burners, and operating valves and holding cups or pitchers while balancing the machine can be tricky. On the positive side, many of the stovetop espresso makers can generate more steam pressure than some of the inexpensive electric machines, but as mentioned, great care must be exercised to avoid burning. Like the Moka, stovetop models with steamers are generally inexpensive ($25 and up).

Though I am not a fan of the espresso brewed by the stovetop machines, I do love the machines themselves. The designs are seemingly endless.

## ELECTRIC ESPRESSO MACHINES

Espresso machines represent the fastest growing segment of the small home appliance market. The espresso boom shows no signs of slowing. The consumer benefits from the many manufacturers who are competing with one another to put the best machine with the best features on the market at an attractive price. My old top-of-the line Krups that I bought years ago still makes wonderful espresso, but is handily outperformed by the new, and considerably less expensive, Krups Novo.

Electric espresso machines can be divided into three categories: steam, pump and piston. Electric steam machines operate in the manner described earlier; steam pressure forces water through the grounds. Pump machines incorporate a pump to force water quickly and at far greater pressure through the grounds and into the cup. Piston machines use a piston which is driven by the manipulation of a lever. The piston machines also operate with substantially greater pressure than steam machines. The new thermal block machines are another type of pump machine. But instead of a boiler, they use a "thermal block" to heat water. Pump and piston machines both operate at a pressure of approximately nine to ten atmospheres. Thermal block machines operate at a pressure of about fourteen to sixteen atmospheres. By comparison, steam machines operate at a pressure of about four to six atmospheres. The three to six atmosphere difference between steam machines and pump and piston machines is about 44 to 88 pounds per square inch. The difference between steam machines and a thermal block machine is about 117 to 176 pounds per square inch, a substantial difference when you consider the resistance offered is provided by approximately two level tablespoons of ground coffee. The increased pressure causes the precisely heated water to surge through the grounds more quickly and uniformly, thereby lessening the possibility of damage to the delicate flavor oils that are the heart and soul of espresso. The optimum water temperature for brewing espresso is approximately 192°F to 198°F. Hotter, the coffee is scalded. Cooler, some flavor is left behind.

The optimum combination of temperature and pressure can be achieved only with a pump or piston machine. These machines heat water by one of two methods: by a boiler or by a thermal block. Boilers are used in the vast majority of home espresso machines. Boilers contain a coil element that heats water the same way electric boilers have heated water for decades. Rather than heating water by contact with an element submerged in a boiler, the thermal block employs a coiled water duct for the same purpose. The water is forced through the duct by a pump, and simultaneously heated. The thermal block itself looks like a waffle or a space age radiator, proving that technology has not ignored the espresso machine. Precise heat control is achieved by both boiler and thermal block machines, with the thermal block offering instant warm-up. Thermal block machines are marketed most widely by Krups and on a lesser scale by the Swiss company, Rotel.

## WHAT TO LOOK FOR WHEN BUYING A MACHINE

It is important to determine what features you want in a machine. As you add features, you add cost. My recommendation is that you buy the best possible machine that you can afford if you want espresso that most closely resembles that prepared by a commercial machine. If you don't already have a burr grinder, use an inexpensive blade grinder until you can afford a good burr grinder. Upgrading a grinder is easier than upgrading an espresso machine.

Many people outgrow steam machines very quickly as their expertise and appreciation of espresso increases. If you can afford a pump or piston machine instead of one that operates on steam pressure, please buy it. Your taste buds will thank you and the ease of operation and performance offered by the pump and piston machines will ensure that they will get used, rather than sit on a shelf.

When shopping for an espresso machine, just as is the case for an electric drip coffee maker, wattage is an important feature. Look for a machine of at least 750 to preferably 900 watts and over. Wattage means power. A machine can offer steaming times in excess of ten minutes, but if the power is insufficient you will be left frustrated when trying to foam milk. Generally, in machines of less than 750 watts, performance suffers. As wattage increases, steaming power increases and warm-up time decreases, as does the time you have to wait between cups when brewing multiple cups.

Added steaming time and power is an obvious benefit to those who have had problems getting milk to foam. The difficulty people have had in trying to foam milk has caused more than a few to bury their espresso machines in the back of a cupboard, never to be used again. There has been a very welcome major innovation in

home espresso machines. The aerating steam wand has arrived making the process of foaming milk a joy. The wand has been available in commercial machines for years. If you have ever waited for your cappuccino or latte in an espresso bar, jealously eyeing the foam created so effortlessly, wipe your tears away. The trick may have been accomplished with one of these wands. Although commercial machines have significantly greater steaming power than home machines, foaming milk with them still requires some skill if an aerating wand is not used. Aerating wands inject air into the milk along with steam, generating tiny bubbles that cause foam to rise effortlessly in the pitcher. With an aerating wand, foaming milk is now such a simple task that anyone capable of submerging the wand in a pitcher of milk can do it. If effortless foaming appeals to you as much as it does to me, ask your retailer for an aerating wand when shopping for your machine. They are widely available and as any frustrated foamer that has tried one will tell you, it is a most valuable feature.

The water capacity of the machine really becomes a factor only if you are not able to refill it during operation. Those machines having a combination water tank and boiler require cooling before they can be refilled, a feature that can be inconvenient. A tank that can hold a large amount of water isn't as important as you might think. I fill my machine with only a little extra water than I will need, and add more as needed. If I am brewing a number of cups for friends or guests, I remove the tank and refill it as I go, or keep a pitcher of fresh water next to the machine. *Never* operate your machine without water. Major damage can occur if you do so. If you buy a machine with a removable water tank, it will be a very simple operation to empty it when you are through brewing and will eliminate the possibility of your water becoming stale. Water does get stale. If you don't believe that it does, put some water in a glass, let it sit a couple of days, then taste it. Always use good, fresh water. If your tap water is unpleasant to drink, the espresso you make with it isn't going to be much better. Better to use bottled water. If your machine has a combination boiler and water tank, remember to empty it before you put it away and *only* when it has cooled. With a machine that has a separate boiler, run the water that remained in the boiler from the previous use through the machine before brewing. In doing so, you will expel the stale water, replacing it with fresh; the discharged water will serve the purpose of preheating your filter holder as well as your cups.

Look for machines that give you the choice of brewing only one or two cups instead of those that require you to brew four at a time. You can waste a lot of coffee if you want only a cup or two. Although you will see a line labelled "2 CUPS" beneath the line that says "4 CUPS" on the filters of some of these machines, don't believe them. They have to be filled to capacity if you want good espresso.

The material used to make your boiler is also important. Boilers are used in all machines with the exception of those using a thermal block to heat water. The water tanks of some machines are also their boilers, making it easy to tell what material the boiler is made from. Aluminum is commonly used for boilers. As aluminum boilers age, they can pit and taint the flavor of the water heated in them. However, with care, pitting can be avoided for a very long time. Stainless steel makes a wonderful boiler material and one that will last indefinitely. Most machines using a combination water tank and boiler are made of stainless steel, which does not impart flavors to the water. Forged brass boilers are used in some machines and are virtually indestructible. They are also expensive, but in my opinion well worth it if you are a committed fan of espresso.

Many machines have separate thermostats for brewing and steaming. The steaming thermostats significantly raise the temperature of the steam produced (as much as 80°F to 90°F), providing you with a dry steam and prolonging the length of time that you are able to use your wand.

On the subject of steaming, a nice feature to look for is a steam valve that will also allow you to use the wand as a water jet, making Americanos a breeze. If you haven't read the recipe section, Americanos are made by adding hot water to espresso, making it a more flavorful alternative to regularly brewed coffee. Don't think you need a wand that doubles as a water jet to make Americanos. You don't. All you have to do is remove the grounds and filter from the filter holder, replace the filter with a clean and empty one, then run as much hot water into your cup as you need.

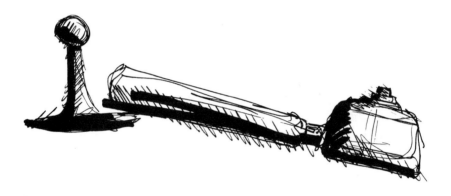

The feature just mentioned is one that is not a necessity. Consider it and others like it, to be an extra. You don't need power windows in a car, but some people are willing to pay a premium for the luxury. Another feature in the same category is the warming tray incorporated into some machines. A nice touch, but all you have to do to warm your cups is run a little hot water into them before brewing. Only you and your budget will be able to decide what "bells and whistles" you want in a machine.

A word on the very expensive home espresso machines. Most are undeniably nice, but the machines in the

$130 to $450 range have reaped the greatest technological benefits of the last few years. Considering the greater competition found in the lower price range, these give the best value for the cost.

## READY TO BUY

Buy a quality name and you will get a quality product. Buy a machine on the reputation and track record of the manufacturer. If a company was making lawn mowers last year and espresso machines this year, there is a better than average chance that you won't be happy with one of its machines.

Before you buy, ask questions. Exhaust the knowledge of the retailer, then do the same with another and another. If friends have espresso machines, taste their espresso and, if you like it, ask them how happy they are with their machines. Read through my recommendations. Go to the library and check through the consumer guides that have reviewed espresso machines. If the same names keep popping up with favorable reviews, you are on your way to making the right choice.

## AT THE STORE

After all the features, prices and reputations have been compared and mulled over, perform the following rather subjective, but essential tests. Feel the machine. Yes, feel it. Run your hands over it. Lift it: is it substantial? Look at the workmanship: how well is the machine finished? Do things fit precisely and does it appear as if care was taken in the manufacture? Take out the filter holder; feel its heft; compare it to the one on the next machine. Remove the water tank (if possible), turn switches, press buttons, remove trays, do anything that might give you a feel for the care taken in the design and manufacture.

Good machines should be works of art. You have to feel good about your machine. You don't make espresso for crowds, you make it for individuals, for romance, for a mood, for thought, for intensity. Espresso, after all, is personal and the machine is an extension of that feeling.

## RECOMMENDATIONS

I will recommend some machines in different price ranges. These are not the only good machines on the market, but are machines that I feel confident in recommending as judged by personal use, or by recommendations of trusted friends who are also aficionados of the brew. I am not including stovetop machines in my list because the advancements and improvements made in recent years to electric steam, pump, or piston machines makes their design, performance and ease of operation overwhelmingly superior.

The prices in parentheses indicate the range of prices found. The low price will often reflect a sale price and if only one price is given, the difference in prices found was negligible.

For those on a budget, the **Krups Il Primo** ($95 to $130) is my choice over the **Krups Mini** ($80 to $110). Krups appliances always seem to finish in the "best buy" categories of consumer tests. Their reputation is well known. Both are steam machines. The Mini will make four cups of espresso. You cannot make single cups. A drawback of the Mini is the inability of the machine to allow you to use the brew and steam functions independently of one another. The Il Primo gives you that capability and is well worth the extra $15 to $20. Both machines must be cooled to refill and both come with the "Perfect Froth" attachment, as do all Krups machines, making frothing milk a simple task.

The **Krups Novo** ($195 to $260) is a very good espresso machine. The Novo is a 1200 watt thermal block machine offering instant warm-up, a 28 ounce removable water tank, and a more than adequate five to six minutes of steaming power. The Novo also comes with the "Perfect Froth" wand now included with all Krups machines. The Novo shows the Krups attention to design and detail. No fluff, just form and function, and a machine that is a pleasure to look at. The **Krups L'Espresso Plus** ($325 to $375) is nearly identical to the Krups Novo. The L'Espresso Plus comes with an instructional video and provides you with the capability of using the Illycaffè espresso pods.

The **Piccola** ($110 to $140) is an 800 watt steam machine made in Italy, that offers complete control over the amount of espresso brewed. The Piccola can provide up to fourteen minutes of continuous steam and gives you the choice of brewing one or two cups at a time. This machine incorporates a back pressure release system to avoid splattering when the filter drum is removed. The Piccola must be cooled to refill.

The **Rotel Espressomat** ($225 to $290) is a wonderful Swiss machine incorporating the thermal block technology, and operates a high 14 to 16 atmospheres of pressure. The machine has a thermostat that raises the temperature of the coiled water duct to 284°F, creating a dry steam. The wand also converts to a water jet, making Americanos an even simpler drink to prepare. Unique to the Espressomat is a separate control for controlling water temperature. The top of the machine doubles as a warming tray for cups. The Espressomat is a 1050 watt machine that reflects the exceptional attention to design that seems to be typical of the Swiss.

Gaggia started making commercial espresso machines in 1949 and their home machines reflect the Gaggia commitment to quality. The **Espresso Gaggia** ($200 to $300) is a 1200 watt pump machine with a large 2.5 liter removable water tank. It has two thermostats (one for brewing, one for steaming), and a steaming time of three to four minutes. In addition to the Gaggia "Turbo Froth" aerating steam wand, you get a cup heating surface on the top of the machine and a chrome over brass filter holder. The filter holder has a wonderful substantial feel to it.

The **Baby Gaggia** ($395 to $475) is a wonderful 1200 watt pump espresso machine capable of producing espresso rivaling that produced by the finest commercial machines. Separate thermostats for brewing and steaming provide you with the correct temperature for brewing as well as elevated temperatures for lengthy steaming. The "Turbo Froth" wand makes frothing milk quick and easy. The wand also acts as a water jet. The Baby Gaggia comes with a large removable water reservoir that can be refilled anytime during operation. The filter holder and delivery group are chrome over forged brass. The Baby Gaggia Bar System consists of the Baby Gaggia coupled with the MDF grinder ($175 to $275) and a matching tray with a drawer for grounds.

Saeco machines are extremely popular in Europe and are now being marketed very heavily in this country. The **Saeco Rio Vapore** ($330 to $385) is a machine that has received many favorable reviews from espresso aficionados. The Rio Vapore operates at 1070 watts and has a 2.9 liter water tank that can be refilled during operation. There are separate thermostats for brewing and steaming.

Rancilio is an Italian company that makes tremendously strong, high quality machines and grinders. The

**Rancilio Sienna** ($250 to $290) is an 1100 watt machine with a powerful electromagnetic pump and a forged brass boiler as well as a forged brass filter holder. The machine has a 45 ounce removable water tank and incorporates separate thermostats for brewing, steaming and safety. The Sienna offers four to five minutes of continuous steam.

The **Rancilio Caffè Rialto** ($390 to $465) is one of my favorite machines. The Rialto is a large 20 pound, 970 watt machine that is pure elegance. The heavy die cast housing of the machine is finished in a porcelain enamel. The machine has a forged brass boiler, brew head, delivery group and filter holder. The powerful electromagnetic pump delivers about six to seven minutes of continuous steam. Like the Sienna, the Rialto comes with a 45 ounce removable water tank and three individual thermostats, one each for brewing, steaming and safety. Couple it with the Rancilio Lido grinder ($130) and you have an espresso maker's delight. For the more extravagant, the Rancilio Rocky ($275) is a 15 pound tempered steel cone grinder that will not only grind your beans to a perfect consistency, but will also measure and dispense them, at the flick of a lever, into the filter holder. Put the machine and grinder on a Rancilio Caffè base ($90 to $100), complete with a sliding grounds tray and you have an espresso bar that will provide you with years and years of espresso bliss. If you have the money and the desire, go ahead, indulge yourself.

The **Saeco Rio Automatica** ($825 to $1000) is a machine for those who want the brewing process to be as quick and neat as possible. Grinding, dosing, brewing, and grounds disposal are all done internally at the touch of a button. I recommend that you ask for a demonstration of its capabilities before you purchase to ensure that it is everything that you are looking for in an espresso machine.

Now for my sentimental favorite. Espresso has always conjured images of gleaming machines with dials and levers, exuding noise and steam, and providing copper roosts for brass eagles with spread wings. The closest most people will get to owning one of these old-fashioned giants is a piston machine like the **La Pavoni Europiccola** ($330 to $450). This downsized version of the machines of old has a nostalgic and romantic look. The Europiccola is solid and very well made. It is expensive, warm-up time is slow, capacity is small, steaming power could be better, and it must be cooled to refill, but I can't help but love it. There is a beauty and drama to making espresso with the Europiccola that is unattainable with the majority of pump machines currently on the market. The long lever operates the piston that forces the hot water through the grounds and into the cup. Not a machine I can recommend for everyone, this is a machine for the incurable romantic. As a child I was in awe of the grandiose cafe machines, but the Europiccola was closer to my size and far less intimidating. It began my love affair with espresso.

# Grind or Hack?

*C*OFFEE BEANS MUST ENDURE MODIFICATIONS FOR YOU TO best exploit the flavor they contain. You've got to break them to appreciate them. But how to do so without damaging the delicate package? Heat destroys the delicate oils of the bean, so the process used to turn the bean into grounds must ideally generate as little heat as possible. The greater the damage, the less flavor in the cup. You have a number of options.

In the beginning, man laid his beans on a rock and mashed them with another, the primitive version of the mortar and pestle. Next came the predecessor of the best of the modern grinders. The millstones that were used to turn grains into flour were also used to grind coffee. The millstone of days gone by operated on the same "rock and a hard place" principle as the mortar and pestle, but the consistency of the grind made it far superior. The stones of old have been replaced by metal burrs or plates in the modern grinders and are powered by an electric motor.

## THE IMPORTANCE OF THE GRIND

The correct grind is absolutely essential for good espresso. Too coarse a grind, and the water will rush through producing a weak, insipid cup. Too fine a grind will result in the coffee clogging the holes of your filter, leaving you with little or nothing in your cup. As the grind is essential, it only makes sense that your choice of a grinder is equally as essential. The grind used for espresso is finer than that used for any other brewing method with the exception of the powdery grind used for Turkish coffee. The finer the grind, the greater the likelihood of damage to the volatile flavor oils of the bean. The grinder must be able to produce the correct grind without destroying the flavor contained in the bean.

## WOODEN BOX GRINDERS

There are a number of hand grinders on the market that are beautiful and of very high quality, but most will not consistently provide as fine a grind as is necessary for espresso.

## ELECTRIC MILL GRINDERS

If you want consistently good espresso, you will need to invest in a good electric burr grinder. They provide the best and most consistent grind, but are not inexpensive. It is possible to spend more on a good grinder than you would for the espresso machine itself. A good grinder produces the desired grind without producing the heat that destroys flavor. That means that the burrs and plates themselves must be of very high quality, preferably of tempered steel and as strong as the motor that drives them. The stronger the motor, the less heat generated. As odd as it may sound, weight is a good indicator of motor strength. Grinders that feature cones will give you the most consistent grind and are superior to grinders using plates. Cones remain sharper over time than do plates. Cone grinders generate less heat since they operate at a slower speed. As features and quality increase, so does cost.

mortar and pestle

wooden box

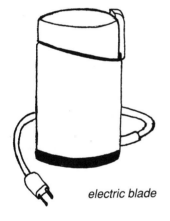

electric blade

electric mill

GRINDERS

There are grinders that only grind beans and those that grind, measure and dispense the beans into your filter holder at the flick of a lever. The **Rancilio Rocky,** the **Gaggia MDF,** and the **Xcell Saeco 2002** are such machines. The Rancilio Rocky and the Gaggia MDF are tempered steel deep cone burr grinders offering professional performance. They are both extremely well made and retail for about $175 to $275. The Saeco is also a tempered steel burr cone grinder of fine quality, retailing for about $155. Rancilio makes the **Lido** cone burr grinder as well that retails for about $100 to $140. Although the Lido doesn't measure the beans and dispense them for you, it does a great job of producing the proper grind for espresso. All three grinders were designed with espresso in mind, but are not the only good quality grinders of such design, so shop around.

Logic dictates that the best machine for a job is one that is designed with that job in mind. Of the mill grinders that were not designed for espresso but still produce a decent grind, you might want to try the **Xcell Emide KM51** that retails for about $60, or the **Bosch MKM700070** that retails for about $90.

## BLADE GRINDERS

If you can afford it, please buy a good burr grinder. However, if your budget requires a $20 rather than a $120 investment, you can't beat the inexpensive blade grinder. Blade grinders are more like choppers than grinders or mills. Coffee is placed in a hopper that houses propeller-like blades connected to an electric motor. A cover is placed over the hopper, a switch is turned causing the blades to spin at high speed, hacking the coffee to pieces. The size of the grind is determined by how long you leave the machine running. After about thirty seconds the coffee is reduced to a size that just bounces off the blades and doesn't get any smaller. With practice you will be able to produce an adequate grind.

Maligned for producing heat and for imprecise grind texture, these machines are very inexpensive ($20 and up) and are incredibly sturdy. I have had one for well over ten years, and have punished it beyond belief by grinding a variety of items, but it keeps running. If only coffee were as impervious to harm. Sadly it is not, and care must be taken to avoid heating the coffee, since the blade process generates heat. About 25 seconds of grinding is all that is necessary for espresso. Never fill your blade grinder to more than half of its capacity. The result will be a more uniform grind. Wipe clean the bowl and cover of your grinder after each use to prevent a build-up of oils from the coffee. And remember to stir the grounds before you use them, eliminating any lumps that may have formed.

The unorthodox style I used for grinding espresso with one of these machines will not be found on their instruction sheets. It arose out of frustration. I was tired of pouring out the larger particles and scraping out the powder that was caked on the walls of the hopper. I placed some beans in the grinder, and as it was running, I shook the grinder as an angry bartender would shake a cocktail shaker. Feeling much better, I opened the grinder to find a more consistent grind, not a perfect one, but a useable one. If you decide that you would like to use this method for grinding, make sure you hold all the parts of the grinder *securely* together, with both hands.

Three of the good blade grinders currently on the market are the **Krups 203,** the **Bosch MKM6003US,** and the **Braun KSM2.** All are priced between $22 and $30.

An important note about blade grinders. They work best when new. Their blades will become dull with use. The irregular grind produced by dull blades is of no use for espresso. If the blades of your grinder have dulled, either replace them or have them sharpened.

Please note: Most grocery store grinders will not produce the correct grind required for espresso even when placed on their finest setting. In addition, preground canned espresso tends to be more coarsely ground than the ideal grind for espresso.

## *AN OPINION*

Good electric burr grinders are expensive. But there is hope. The dramatic growth experienced in recent years by the home espresso market has not gone unnoticed. The attention of the manufacturers will be placed on the segments of the market that offer the greatest potential for growth. As an example, the top of the line Krups Espresso Plus that retailed for $375 in 1985

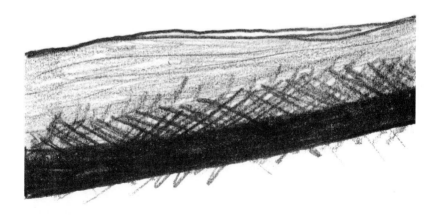

is now outperformed by the current $240 Krups Novo. Increased demand leads to greater competition, and greater competition leads to better quality and lower prices at the consumer level. As the manufacturers' espresso machine market shares level out, the emphasis will shift to other areas. The grinder is a niche that is going to get attention.

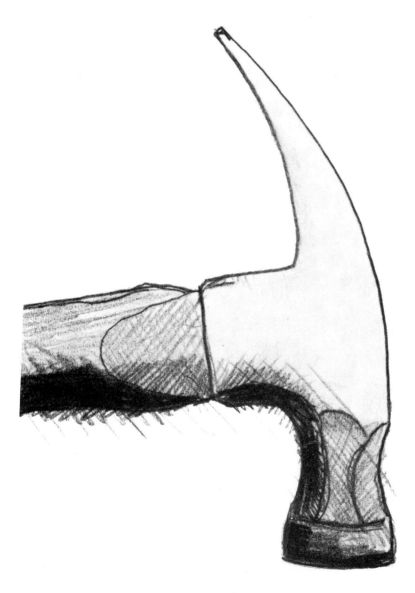

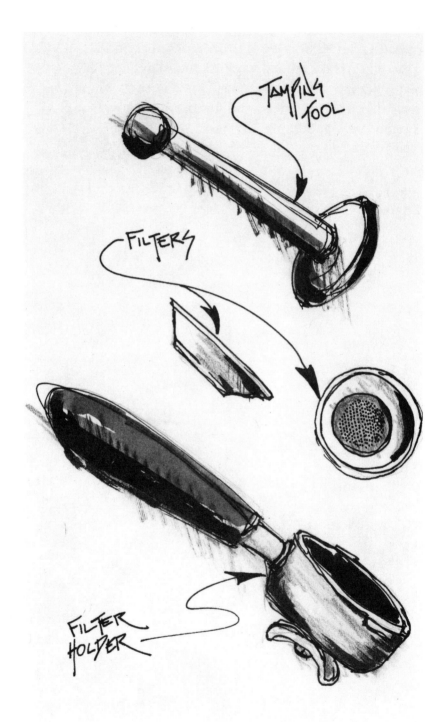

TAMPING TOOL

FILTERS

FILTER HOLDER

# Brewing Espresso

*T*HIS IS A STEP BY STEP GUIDE DESIGNED TO HELP YOU make perfect espresso using your home machine. Set aside some time because you will need to practice. Read this chapter completely before you start brewing. Doing so will help give you an idea of what we are trying to accomplish. Follow the directions carefully and by the time you get to the end of this chapter you will be on your way to making a perfect cup of espresso, easily, every time.

## AN ESPRESSO PRIMER

Espresso is terribly misunderstood. Many who have never tried espresso condemn it as a bitter and offensive brew. Regrettably, many of the espressos served to me in restaurants over the years would fall into that category. Fortunately, a Mediterranean heritage taught me what good espresso was before I ever ordered one in a restaurant. Don't assume that the person who prepares your espresso knows what he is doing. The machine may be the finest in the world, but if the operator doesn't understand the process, all hope is lost. Espresso should not be bitter or harsh. It should be smooth, delicious and extraordinarily aromatic. Espresso is my favorite way to take advantage of what the coffee bean has to offer.

Espresso is more complex than other methods of brewing. You need specialized equipment and a knowledge of preparation. But with a little effort, you will be rewarded with flavor much richer than possible with any other brewing method. Once you learn the basics, you will find it easy to make a cup of espresso rather than to brew a pot of regular coffee. Let's get started.

## *THE MACHINE*

Your machine must be capable of producing the proper pressure and temperature necessary for brewing espresso. Brewing technique will vary depending upon the design and performance of your machine. What works with one may not work with another. This guide is designed to ensure your success with any espresso machine. To learn more about the operation of espresso machines, or if you are considering the purchase of one, refer to the "Espresso Machine" section of this book.

## *THE ROAST*

The beans must be fresh. For our purposes select a dark roast, preferably one made especially for espresso. The espresso process is one that accentuates the acids in coffee and for that reason the darker roasts, which are typically low in acid, are used most often and produce classic espresso. Light roasts tend to produce a bitter brew. As discussed in the chapter on the bean, espresso roasts are most commonly blends of different beans. However, once you learn the basics, experiment with straight coffees (those that are not blends) to better understand the particular characteristics of different coffees. Some straight coffees make excellent espresso. Full City or Viennese roasts of Colombian Supremo and Ethiopian Yergacheffe are two of my favorite alternatives.

Remember, roasts are not standardized so choose by bean color and luster. I recommend that you start with the lightest of the dark roasts and go lighter or darker as your taste dictates.

## THE GRIND

The only grind for espresso is one that is even and of a fine, gritty texture, but not a powder. The grains should be roughly the size of grains of sugar, sand, or salt. The problem is that coffee cannot be ground to such precise texture. Coffee ground for espresso has a much softer look, more like pepper ground from a mill. Coincidentally, most pepper mills when placed on their finest setting, produce a grind texture that is nearly perfect for espresso and one that will help you to better visualize the proper grind that is so important. I don't recommend grinding coffee in a pepper mill (it would take about ten minutes to do enough for a cup). However, if you do have one, use it for the starting point in your search for the perfect espresso grind. Another option is to ask a roaster for a sample grind.

Owners of certain Krups, Gaggia and DeLonghi machines can take an easy way out: Illycaffè, Italy's best espresso roaster, sells espresso pre-ground and packaged in individual pods designed to fit the specially built filter holders of the machines mentioned above. Place a pod in the filter holder and you are ready to brew. The cost is about $10.95 for 18 pods. They work well, are becoming increasingly more available where the machines are sold and offer the utmost in ease. As of this writing the pods are available in two roasts, and are available with or without caffeine. For more information about the pods and the location of the retailer nearest you, call Illycaffè at (800) 872-4559.

The correct grind is of utmost importance. Most espresso bars will adjust their grinders several times daily; many adjust their grinders to compensate for prevailing humidity. The reason they do is that the bean is very susceptible to changes in humidity. A specific grind may be too porous on days of low humidity and too dense in more humid weather. It is inevitable that grinders will become dull with use. Replace, or have sharpened, the burrs, plates, or blades of your grinder if you notice that the grind produced is becoming less consistent. I recommend that if you use a burr grinder, set it at its coarsest setting and run the grinder to expel any grounds that may have been left from an earlier use. If possible, a small brush should be used occasionally to clean the burrs themselves. Don't set and forget the grinders. They easily lose their adjustment. If that makes grinding sound intimidating, understand that with practice you will be able to consistently grind beans to the proper texture with ease. Too coarse a grind and the water will gush around the grounds and deliver a weak, tasteless liquid to your cup. Too fine a grind will result in a clogged filter with little or no water passing through. The filter is the perforated basket used to hold the grounds for brewing. Espresso is made through a unique process that forces water through the packed grounds as opposed to letting the water drip by force of gravity on and around the loose grounds. When done properly, the flavor oils emulsify with the espresso itself, rather than ride on top of it as they do in regularly brewed coffee.

## TAMPING

The grind is married to the tamp. Tamping is the name for the compacting and packing of the grounds in the filter. A tamping tool is included with most machines and on others a protrusion exists on the machine for that purpose. My preference is for a flat-bottomed tamping tool as opposed to one that is slightly convex. The tamp should be flat and level to ensure the even flow of water through the coffee. If your tool is rounded, try the bottom of a glass or the bottom of a flat measuring cup. I use two metal measuring cups, one 1/4 cup and the other 1/3 cup. Both have the same diameter base. No matter what you use to tamp, the fit must be perfect and the bottom smooth. Initially, use whatever came with the machine and, if unsatisfactory, try something else.

More important than the shape of your tamping tool is the tamping itself. The grind must be tamped precisely. A firm, even pressure must be used. The coarser the grind, the firmer the tamp. A single espresso should be made with about six and one half to seven grams of coffee, a little less than two level tablespoons. A pound of coffee should yield about sixty single cups of espresso, so a nominal investment should give you the practice you need to make good espresso.

## GETTING READY TO BREW

Ideally, a single serving of espresso should be 1-1/2 to 1-3/4 ounces. Brewing more from a single measure of grounds will result in a thin and very bitter brew. Over-brewing is one of the most common mistakes made when brewing espresso. Remember that the process forces water through the grounds under high pressure causing almost instantaneous contact with each grain of coffee. The delicate essence of the coffee is extracted very quickly; prolonging the contact between water and coffee by extending the brewing time draws out unpleasant bitter chemicals and destroys flavor and aroma. 1-1/2 ounces of espresso should be brewed in 20 to 25 seconds. If you want two cups of espresso and your machine came with

*Begin by placing the filter in the filter holder, add the coffee, then tamp.*

two filters, use the larger filter and brew the two cups in the same amount of time using twice the coffee. Look at the number of holes in each filter. Notice that there are more holes in the larger filter. The volume of water passing through the larger filter in the same amount of time will be greater than that through the smaller one.

Take 1/2 cup of the dark-roast beans (about 1-1/2 ounces) and grind them to the texture described earlier. Try to make the grind as consistent as possible. Place what you grind in a small bowl and stir the grounds with a spoon to ensure an even, loose mixture. Note the texture. You now have enough grounds to brew about six cups of espresso. Put the grounds aside and keep reading.

Use demitasse cups (about 1-1/2 to 3 ounces) for espresso. A shot of espresso is overwhelmed by a regular cup or mug and will be much more enjoyable when properly presented. Demitasse spoons will complete your espresso service. Use cups with a capacity of about six ounces if you are preparing cappuccinos or lattes. A wide range of designs in both cups and spoons will accommodate any taste.

Make your machine ready for brewing. Do this only after having carefully read the manufacturer's instructions for your machine. Follow all guidelines for operation and safety. Now that your machine is ready for brewing, attach your filter holder with the basket in place to the machine and place a cup under the holder. Use your brew switch to run some hot water through the holder and into the cup, preheating both filter holder and cup. Leave the water in the cup until you are ready to brew. A two ounce shot glass can be a great help in determining the amount of espresso brewed. If used, preheat the same way you would a cup. Preheating is necessary since a serving of espresso is very small and a cold cup can cool it very quickly as can a cold filter holder. Never pour your espresso into a cold cup, as it will "shock" the coffee and change the flavor. And never run hot water through your machine when the filter holder is not in place. The water is near boiling temperature and can burn you severely.

*Preheating is accomplished by filling your cups with hot water prior to brewing*

Water is the main ingredient of espresso; it must be fresh and drawn from the cold tap. If your water is hard, artificially softened, or doesn't taste good when you drink it, you are better off using bottled or filtered water. By running water through your machine to preheat your cup or cups, you also run previously heated water through the boiler, enabling you to brew with fresh water. Obviously, if you have a machine with an accessible boiler (as opposed to one that is fed from a separate tank) you should empty it between uses to prevent brewing with stale water. Read the instructions that came with your machine to see if the manufacturer recommends draining your machine between uses as a point of maintenance.

Your machine probably came with two filters or baskets, one for a single cup, and one for two cups. The smaller of the two is for single cups. Take that filter and place it in the filter holder, taking care not to burn yourself on the preheated filter holder. If your machine did not come with two filter holders, you must always brew to the capacity of the filter. The following brewing instructions are for single cups; alter the amounts given according to quantity brewed to be able to fully benefit from this guide.

If your machine came with a coffee measure, use it to measure seven grams (a little less than two level tablespoons) of the coffee you have set aside and fill the filter. If your machine did not come with a measure and you don't have a measuring spoon, fill the filter just slightly more than level. Tap the side of the filter holder against the tamping tool to even the grounds before you tamp. With a firm, even pressure, tamp the coffee to a point a

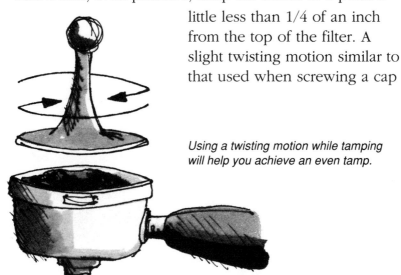

little less than 1/4 of an inch from the top of the filter. A slight twisting motion similar to that used when screwing a cap

*Using a twisting motion while tamping will help you achieve an even tamp.*

*Wipe or brush excess grounds from the rim of the filter and filter holder to ensure a leak-free fit to the machine.*

on a jar will help you to get an even tamp. Tapping the side of the filter holder against the tamping tool will help to distribute any loose grounds that may have accumulated on the sides of the filter. Tamp again to compact the loose grounds. After tamping, brush away any excess coffee from the rim of the filter and filter holder in order to ensure a leak-free fit when attaching the holder to the machine. Make sure the filter holder is attached *securely* to the machine. Don't be afraid to put it on tightly. Water should never be allowed to escape from the seal between the filter holder and machine. Once the filter holder is attached securely to the machine, look at the handle. It should be pointing either straight at you, perpendicular to the body of the machine, or just slightly to the right. If the handle is pointing to the left, either the filter is overloaded or you need to use a firmer tamp.

Espresso should flow smoothly, slowing near the end of the brewing cycle as the grounds expand. Italians call the ideal trickle of espresso the "coda di topo" or "tail of the mouse." If you have never really looked at a mouse's tail or don't think a mouse is that cute, the flow can also be likened to syrup or honey dripping from a spoon. Every cup of espresso should be crowned by a layer of light cinnamon brown, extremely fine foam called "crema." A delicious froth, crema is the mark of a truly fine cup, and is a testament to the skill of the brewer. Trapped inside the delicate crema is the aroma of espresso. Sugar granules sprinkled into a cup of espresso should float momentarily before sinking. Your espresso should be fragrant, rich and robust with a luscious bittersweet, almost chocolaty aftertaste. A good espresso should stay pleasantly on your palate for at least twenty minutes.

*Don't be afraid to use some force when attaching the filter holder to the machine - the fit must be tight.*

## BREWING YOUR ESPRESSO

Now we are ready for brewing. Time yourself as you brew. Activate your brew switch and continue to do so for 20 to 25 seconds after the flow of espresso begins. Brew for 25 seconds if you are using a steam machine and for 20 seconds for all others. Your machine will make a lot of noise; this is normal. If the espresso does not begin to flow within 15 to 20 seconds, stop brewing. Use a coarser grind or a lighter tamp.

## IF YOU HAVE LESS THAN 1-1/2 OUNCES IN YOUR CUP

If at the end of the 20 to 25 second brew time you have considerably less than the desired 1-1/2 ounces (about 3 tablespoons) of espresso in your cup, remove the filter holder and look at the grounds. If the grounds are sloppy and resemble smooth, wet pudding, or if they are wet and rise in gritty peaks, the grind is most likely too fine. The saturated, powdery grounds are clogging the small holes of your filter preventing the flow of espresso. As a last resort, before you grind more coffee, fill your filter with new grounds from the same batch and try an extremely light tamp. If you have little success, grind another 1/2 cup of beans to a coarser consistency.

If the grounds look somewhat solid but slightly wet, press them with a spoon. If the water rises smoothly from the grounds as water rises from under your foot in wet sand, the grind is probably too fine and is clogging the filter holes in the same way as the wet, sloppy grounds described above. Knock the grounds out of the filter. Ideally, they should fall out in one piece or break into two or three pieces. If they fall out like wet mud, try the same solution suggested in the previous paragraph. If you still end up short in your cup, grind another 1/2 cup of beans to a coarser consistency and try again.

If the grounds look and react more like hard-packed, slightly damp dirt, you have probably used too strong a tamp for the grind. Try again using the same grind coupled with a lighter tamp until you get the sought after ounce and a half. Make sure you are not overloading your filter.

## *IF YOU HAVE MORE THAN 1-1/2 OUNCES IN YOUR CUP*

Make sure you are using the single filter. Remove the filter holder from the machine and look at  the grounds. The surface should be smooth, the grounds firm and even. If the grounds look as though they have been through a tropical storm and the filter is not full, you probably didn't use enough coffee. Re-check your method for measuring the grounds and repeat the brewing process.

If you have more than the desired 1-1/2 ounces and the grounds look smooth and firm, repeat the brewing process using a firmer tamp until you end up with the right amount of espresso. If firmer tamps still give you more than 1-1/2 ounces of espresso, the grind is too coarse. Grind another 1/2 cup of beans to a finer texture than before and start over.

## IF YOU HAVE 1-1/2 (OR EVEN 1-3/4) OUNCES IN YOUR CUP

Now you have to move quickly. Smell the espresso. The aroma should be intense without smelling scorched. A smoky aroma is fine and will become more evident as you use a progressively darker roast. Remove the filter holder and look at the grounds. The surface should be smooth, the grounds firm and even. They should have expanded to completely fill any headroom left from tamping. Look for the crema. Remember, crema is an extremely fine foam. It should range in color from a light to a dark tan, depending upon the coffee used, and should cover the espresso.

## IF LITTLE OR NO CREMA, OR CREMA WITH LARGE BUBBLES

Some light roasts will not produce crema, but since we are using a dark roast, the crema should be evident. If it is not, several adjustments may be necessary. The beans must be fresh or you will have little luck in producing consistent crema. If the crema has large bubbles, either too little coffee was used, the tamp was too light, or the grind was too coarse. Make sure you are using the right amount of coffee. Measure more of the grounds and try a firmer tamp. If the crema is still not evident, the grind is probably too coarse. Grind another 1/2 cup of beans to a slightly finer texture, and start again, feeling happy about the fact that you are almost there.

## IF THE CREMA IS THIN AND DARK BROWN

Make sure you are using the right amount of coffee. Try a slightly lighter tamp. If a lighter tamp doesn't solve the problem, grind another 1/2 cup of beans to a slightly coarser texture, and start again.

## IF NOTHING WORKS

If you have followed all the instructions and can't get a good layer of crema, the coffee is either not fresh or is not suitable for espresso. If you can't find a good, fresh espresso blend locally, go to the "Sources" section and call one of the roasters who offers blends specifically made for espresso.

## IF YOU HAVE A SMOOTH CREMA

Congratulations! Now sprinkle some sugar granules on the espresso. If the sugar granules sink quickly without being momentarily buoyed by the espresso, try a slightly finer grind, and adjust the tamp accordingly. Don't change much since you are much closer now than you were in the last paragraph. If the granules float momentarily before sinking, you have achieved the right balance.

Now for the long awaited final test. It should be marvelously aromatic. Taste it. If sour and watery, try a finer grind. If bitter and sour, try a coarser grind. If rich, fragrant and robust, you have succeeded.

Save some of the unused grounds of the ideal grind that gave you your perfect cup and put them in a baggie or clear container for future comparison as a grinding aid.

Make sure you clean your machine after each use. When through brewing, attach the filter holder to the machine and run some water through to clean the perforated screen of the delivery head. Use a small, stiff brush to remove any remaining traces of grounds around the head and gasket. Exercise great care when cleaning the machine since many of the parts will be hot and capable of burning you severely. A machine that is not properly cleaned can ruin the next cup.

## SUMMARY

Brewing espresso is the art of making fine adjustments in your methods to allow for the many variables. You may find the first cup you brew each time will be thrown away and some minor adjustment needed. Once able to obtain consistent results, experiment with grind, tamp, and duration of pour. Different results in flavor can be obtained by varying each of the steps. Try saturating the grounds before brewing. To saturate the grounds, turn your brew switch on and off very quickly, wait a moment, then brew. Experiment until you find the cup that satisfies your own tastes – *that* is the true art of espresso.

Some people do not like the taste of straight espresso. No matter. Whether you like cappuccinos, lattes, mochas, Americanos or any other espresso drink, what you have in front of you is the essential building block for all espresso drinks as well as a versatile ingredient in cooking, as I will show you later in the book. Enjoy, and practice, practice, practice.

# Quick Reference Brewing Guide

## IF AFTER 20 TO 25 SECONDS YOU HAVE:

**Less than 1-1/2 ounces:**

*use a lighter tamp*
*use a coarser grind*

**More than 1-1/2 ounces:**

*use a firmer tamp*
*use more coffee*
*use a finer grind*

**1-1/2 OUNCES**

## LOOK FOR CREMA

**Little or no crema, or crema with large bubbles:**

*use more coffee*
*use a firmer tamp*
*use a finer grind*

**Thin, or thin and dark brown crema:**

*use more coffee*
*use a lighter tamp*
*use a coarser grind*

**Smooth crema:**

*Enjoy!*

## USING THIS GUIDE

*Each step is a separate solution. Perform each in the order given. Use only* **fresh** *coffee. Once you have learned to brew a good cup using a coffee roasted and blended specifically for espresso, experiment with other coffees to find those that best satisfy your tastes - the brewing process is the same. Remember, a fresh espresso blend is no further away than the "Sources" section of this book.*

# Frothing Milk

*F*ROTHING MILK. THESE ARE TWO WORDS THAT STRIKE fear into the hearts of many. Without the splendid foam of frothed and steamed milk there can be no cappuccinos. No warm, creamy, insulating cap to the wonderful espresso that you have created. For those of you new to the world of espresso, frothing is the process of creating hot, foamed milk with the steam wand of your espresso machine, used in drinks such as cappuccinos, as well as lattes, mochas and the like. Heating by steaming alters the proteins of the milk in a way that creates a distinctive, unforgettable flavor. Keep the milk out of the microwave; put the pan away, and start steaming.

Heating milk by steaming is easy. All you have to do is submerge the tip of the steam wand in a pitcher of milk and open the steam valve, leaving it open until the milk reaches the desired temperature. Creating foam is an entirely different matter.

If you have tried frothing milk for a cappuccino or latte, and have ended up disappointed with a container of hot milk, burned hands and no foam, smile.

There is hope.

# MAGIC WANDS

There are ways to easier frothing. One is the solution many manufacturers of commercial machines have been using to accommodate the volume of froth required to keep up with the demand at espresso bars. The steaming wands of their machines are designed to inject air along with the steam into the milk. As the steam heats the milk, the injected air forms bubbles that rise to the top, and you have only to worry about the temperature of the milk so as to avoid scorching. These special wands have found their way to the home espresso machine. Home machines have considerably less power than their commercial counterparts; you won't make froth as easily as they can, but be heartened by the fact that you can easily produce enough froth for your purposes. The actual designs of these wands will differ from manufacturer to manufacturer, but all operate by the same principle.

If you have not yet purchased an espresso machine and you find this a worthwhile feature, be sure to mention it to your retailer. Enough manufacturers are making machines with these wands that you will have a large variety of machines to choose from in all price ranges. They will make your milk foaming much easier.

But what if you already own a machine and it doesn't have such a wand? For those of you who own Krups machines with a steaming wand that isn't an aerating wand, you have the easiest option. Krups has come out with an attachment exclusively for their machines that allows you to make perfect froth easily. The attachment is called "Perfect Froth." Just slide the rubber boot of the "Perfect Froth" attachment over your existing Krups steam wand, and you are ready to froth. Look for it where Krups machines are sold. It should cost between $7 and $9, and is well worth the money. Krups is the only company I am aware of that makes an aerating froth attachment that can be retrofitted to their machines. If your machine is not a Krups, but your steam attachment is the same size and shape as those found on Krups machines, it should work just as well as on a Krups machine. Since Krups says it should be used only on their machines, using it on a machine that is not a Krups would obviously have to be done at your own risk.

## *STEAMERS*

Now, what do you do if you already have an espresso machine, don't want to buy another, yet still want perfect froth? You have two options. The first, and most expensive, is to buy a machine that is made solely for the purpose of generating steam for milk. Milk steamers have been around for a long time, but until now most left a lot to be desired.

Stovetop steamers can generate more steam than some electric machines, but can be tricky to work with due to the external heat source. If you would like a stovetop steamer, a variety of models are available for between $40 and $50. A much better choice, albeit a more expensive one, is an electric steamer. Recently, two steamers have appeared on the market that work beautifully. They are the **Cappuccino Pronto!** by Maxim, and the **Café Cappuccino** by Salton, the parent company of Maxim. They retail in the $70 range. If you have trouble frothing milk using the steam wand on your machine you might want to buy one of these steamers.

If steamers aren't for you, but you still want to froth milk, read the following directions.

# THE ROAD TO FINE FOAMING

Start out with *cold* milk. First place the pitcher containing the milk in a bowl of ice water or in the freezer for a short time to make it as cold as possible. Doing so will make frothing the milk a simpler task. Cold milk froths more easily than warm milk, so never heat the milk first. First you froth, then you steam heat the milk. Use whole, 2% or nonfat milk. The difference is minimal. It has been my experience that nonfat milk froths the easiest, so that is a good place to start. The froth created by nonfat milk tends to be stiff and dry. Two percent produces a smooth foam, and one that lasts longer than nonfat. It is my personal favorite. Whole milk requires a little more skill (but not much), but each can be frothed with a little practice. If you prefer a stiffer foam, let the milk stand for a couple of minutes. If you prefer your foam smooth and creamy, use it immediately. Always stir your foam before serving to eliminate any large bubbles that may have formed.

Use only a clean stainless steel pitcher, not glass, ceramic, or any other material. I can easily steam milk in a stainless steel pitcher, but have had mixed results with glass. A stainless steel pitcher made for frothing milk will cost between $7 and $15. Buy a small, short pitcher as opposed to a large or tall one. You will want to froth about 1 to 1-1/2 cups of milk at a time. The limited steam time on some machines will prevent you from frothing more at a single session. The other reason for a small, short pitcher has to do with the length of the steaming wand. Once frothed, the wand must be able to be completely submerged in the remainder of the milk in order to heat it. The milk will roughly double or triple in volume when frothed, so choose your pitcher size accordingly.

When you are ready to start, before you put the wand into the milk, submerge it into a container of water and turn your steam valve on for a short time in order to expel any water that might have accumulated in the wand. Once the steam has started in the water, turn the valve off, remove the container of water and replace it with the pitcher of *cold* milk. Make sure the wand is deep in the milk before you open your steam valve. Open the valve completely for optimum steaming power. As soon as you open the steam valve, lower the pitcher until the tip of the wand is just beneath the surface of the milk.

If the pitcher is held too low, the wand will be too high in the milk causing one of two things to happen. Either the bubbles formed will be too large and will disappear quickly, or you will splatter milk all over the place. If the milk is hot, that can be a very painful experience. With the wand too high in the milk you will hear an irregular, sputtering sound – not the sound you want to hear.

If the pitcher is held too high, the wand will be too low in the milk and all you will hear is a low, beautiful, smooth, rumbling sound, not unlike the sound a jet makes as it passes you by on takeoff, but with a much warmer note to it. But you will have no foam. With the wand too deep in the milk, no matter how long you keep steaming, you will not have foam, but you will have scorched milk unsuitable for anything but the drain.

You want to hold the tip of the wand just low enough in the milk to allow air to be pulled into the milk by the force of the steam, creating the tiny bubbles that will rise to the top and become foam. Starting with the wand deep in the milk, you want to lower the pitcher slowly until the low, steady rumbling sound is replaced by

*Begin by submerging the steam wand in the milk. Open the valve to begin steaming only when the tip of the wand is **completely** submerged.*

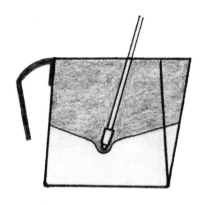

*Lower the pitcher until the tip of the steaming wand is just under the surface of the milk. When you hear an irregular sputtering sound, raise the pitcher until the irregular sound **just** disappears.*

*When you have finished frothing, lower the wand into the pitcher to heat the remainder of the milk to the desired temperature. Turn the steam valve **off** before removing the wand from the milk.*

one of a higher pitch, but still smooth and steady. If, as you are lowering the pitcher, the sound becomes irregular and almost piercing, raise the pitcher until it smooths out again. Raising or lowering the pitcher should always be a slow, smooth, almost imperceptible motion.

At the beginning of the steaming process, when the milk has no foam at all, you should be able to see a small depression in the milk caused by the force of the steam. The depression should disappear as the foam begins to rise. You should be able to just detect a *steady* staccato of tiny bubbles being furiously injected into the milk. As the foam begins to rise, keep the wand just under the surface of the milk.

Keeping the tip of the wand just under the surface of the remaining milk when you can't see the surface of the milk can be challenging, but is easier than it sounds. You have to use your ears. Too low in the milk and the rumbling mentioned previously will return, though muffled more and more by the foam. Too high, and large bubbles will begin forming on the surface. A muffled sputtering will be heard. Just right, and the ideal sound described earlier will become steadily fainter, but no less smooth.

## HOW HOT?

After you have developed a head of foam on the milk, or if you just want to heat milk to add to your es-presso, you need to submerge the tip of the steam wand deep into the milk until the desired temperature is reached. At that time, turn the steam wand off *before* removing it from the milk. Place the wand back into the container of water and turn the steam valve on again to clean out any milk that may have entered the wand. Do not skip this last step. The health and happiness of your wand as well as your boiler may depend upon it. Then, taking care not to burn, take a damp cloth or scrub sponge and wipe the steam wand clean before the milk hardens. If the milk is not wiped immediately, it will be nearly impossible to remove later. A little baking soda on a damp cloth helps to remove stubborn deposits left on the wand, but remember to run some steam through after doing so in order to prevent any of the baking soda from clogging the jet of the wand.

How hot is hot enough? That really is a matter of personal preference. I prefer the milk to be from 140°F to 160°F. Some prefer hotter and some prefer cooler. Hotter than 170°F and you take the chance of scorching the milk. Cooler than 140°F and you will be cooling the espresso too much.

So how can you tell how hot your milk has become? There are several ways. The first is to keep one hand on the pitcher (if your steam valve allows) until it becomes so hot that you can touch it only for a very brief time without burning. If you have a low threshold of pain or dislike burning as much as I do, you should opt for the next method, a thermometer that can measure temperatures greater than those you want for your milk. A candy thermometer with the temperature dial on top works very well for that purpose. When you measure the temperature, be sure to keep the end of the thermometer in the milk as opposed to in the foam. The temperature of the foam will be a little less than that of the milk due to the air content of the foam. The third method involves your ears. With some experience and practice, you will be able to determine the proper temperature of the milk by the deepening pitch produced by the wand when deep in the milk. Remember, if it is too hot to touch, it is too hot to drink.

You should now have an understanding of how tc froth milk; practice will give you an ear and feel for the process. You will be creating your own perfect froth in less time than you think. As with brewing: practice, practice, practice.

# HOW TO MAKE ESPRESSO DRINKS

**W**ITH THE DIVERSITY THAT ESPRESSO HAS TO OFFER, there is a drink to please every espresso drinker. Experiment with different roasts, omit ingredients, add new ones, vary proportions and take notes on what you have changed. I recommend using ristretto rather than full shots of espresso for lattes and cappuccinos to prevent the milk from overpowering the flavor of the coffee. A ristretto is made by cutting short the flow of espresso before a full ounce is poured. Any of the recipes can be made with decaffeinated coffee, and regular coffee can be substituted for Americanos. Heavy glass cups or mugs can give a nice effect to layered espresso drinks. Tailor the drinks to reflect your own tastes and the individual espresso experience.

## INGREDIENTS

### Whipped Cream

Use whipped cream that you have whipped yourself. Canned whipped cream will melt very quickly and will not give you the superior texture that homemade whipped cream does. It takes just a few minutes. If you like whipped cream that is fairly stiff, add a little sugar to it before whipping. If you like it wet and smooth, whip it until soft, not stiff, peaks form. Whipped cream can be delicately flavored by adding a few drops of one of the various extracts, including mint, vanilla or almond.

*Spices*

Always use fresh spices that you grate or grind yourself just before using. The difference a little freshly grated nutmeg can make over that bought ground is remarkable. If the recipe calls for whole clove, use whole clove and not ground. Try adding a cinnamon stick to your lattes or mochas as a complement to ground cinnamon on top.

Sprinkle a little cinnamon, allspice, or nutmeg on your cappuccinos and lattes, and experiment further with different spices. Cardamom is a little known spice that goes very well with lattes. Cardamom complements cinnamon and nutmeg quite well, and is also very nice on its own. It has a slight lemony taste with just a hint of eucalyptus. Usually sold already ground, a gourmet section of a store or an East Indian grocery may have whole cardamom in seed or pod form. It is very strong, so use only a dash if ground, and, if bought in whole form, crush only a few small seeds for your lattes.

*Toppings*

Everyone knows about cinnamon and nutmeg, but many don't realize that other spices such as vanilla come powdered. Take a trip down the spice aisle of the grocery store, or that of a gourmet food shop. Try a little grated orange peel or some chocolate chips on top of your whipped cream, or in a cappuccino or latte as well. The chips will sink in a cappuccino or latte, but finding them at the bottom of the cup is a treat. Cocoa powder makes a great topping. When buying cocoa powder, remember to buy only the highest quality cocoa powder, unsweetened. Try sweetening it with powdered sugar.

### Chocolate

Try some other than those you usually buy; there are some great chocolates to be found. Grating your own chocolate is very easy and noticeably enhances the flavor of a cappuccino, latte, or mocha. To grate chocolate, you need to refrigerate it first. Blocks of chocolate work best for grating. When thoroughly refrigerated, hold the chocolate using a cloth or paper towel to avoid transferring the heat of your hand to the chocolate. Grate the chocolate over a sheet of wax paper. If the room is warm, keep the grated chocolate in the refrigerator until needed.

### Flavored Syrups

The many different flavored syrups used to flavor lattes can also be used to flavor steamed milk without espresso. Steamed milk has a different flavor to it than milk heated by any other method; try offering some flavored steamed milk to those who don't want any espresso in their drinks. Almond, strawberry, hazelnut, vanilla, coconut, blueberry, mango, kiwi, tangerine, cherry, banana, papaya and raspberry are only a few of the many fruit and nut flavors available. If you have trouble finding the syrups locally, look in the "Sources" section for roasters offering Torani brand syrups.

Almond syrup is also called orgeat. The word orgeat is from the French *orge*, meaning barley. Orgeat (pronounced OR-zhaht) was a preparation extracted from barley and almonds, used in drinks or for medicinal purposes. Why it is now used to identify almond syrup is beyond me.

Most flavored syrups are pre-sweetened. If you would prefer non-sweetened flavorings, buy extracts. Pure extracts are best since the heat of coffee intensifies flavors, and any shortcomings will be amplified.

The best hot chocolate and cocoa is made with steamed milk. Use chocolate flavored syrup, but don't overlook cocoa powder with plain or vanilla sugar added. Remember to make a paste from the cocoa powder and a little steamed milk before adding it to the cup to prevent lumps from forming.

### Vanilla Sugar

Vanilla is such a wonderful addition to lattes and mochas. Vanilla flavored sugar can be used to impart a flavor that is not overpowering, but still very noticeable. To make vanilla sugar, put one or two vanilla pods in a quart-sized jar. Fill the jar with sugar and cover tightly. In a few days, the sugar will have been flavored by the vanilla and can then be used in place of plain sugar. Replenish the sugar as you use it. A vanilla pod will last many months in a tightly closed container.

## THE ORDER OF THINGS

Espresso is most flavorful when fresh. Steam or froth the milk for espresso drinks before brewing the espresso. Spoon foam and pour milk over espresso in the cup rather than adding espresso to the milk.

## TRADITIONAL ESPRESSO DRINKS

With the exception of Americanos, straight shot espresso is usually drunk black, and often with sugar. Some like to flavor their espresso. Try a bit of cocoa powder, vanilla sugar, or a few drops of a flavored syrup, such as almond or hazelnut.

As mentioned earlier, classic espresso is made from dark roast coffee, but can be made from any properly ground coffee. You may enjoy using one coffee for straight espresso and another for cappuccinos or mochas, so don't limit yourself to one coffee, roast or blend.

## Solo –

A single shot (approximately 1-1/2 ounces) of **espresso**, usually quaffed in a single gulp while at its flavorful peak, before it cools.

## Doppio –

Two full shots (approximately 3 ounces) of **espresso** for true lovers of the brew.

## Espresso Ristretto –

The flow of **espresso** is cut short leaving less than an ounce in your cup. A very intense cup.

## Espresso con Panna –

A shot of **espresso** topped with a dollop of **whipped cream**. Beat the cream until it forms soft, wet peaks, then put a spoonful on the **espresso**.

## Espresso Romano –

A single shot of **espresso** served with a twist or slice of **lemon** on the side. Italians insist that the addition of the lemon is not Italian, but never the less the name stands. Many feel the lemon upsets the balance of flavor.

# *CAPPUCCINO*

Cappuccinos are often misunderstood. *The Random House Dictionary* defines cappuccino as: "A hot beverage consisting of espresso coffee and steamed milk, often served with powdered cinnamon and topped with whipped cream." All they missed were the maraschino cherries and multi-colored chocolate sprinkles that are added to coffee in all too many restaurants and sold as cappuccinos. Cherries, chocolate sprinkles, and whipped cream have no place in cappuccino.

The name cappuccino is said to have come from the chocolate color of the robes worn by the Capuchin monks, or from their hoods, which are often likened to the insulating "cap" of the espresso formed by the foamed milk. No one knows for sure, so feel free to speculate.

Just what defines a cappuccino is often a matter of debate. It can vary from country to country, region to region, state to state, city to city, cafe to cafe, and person to person. In the interest of freedom of choice, two variations are included here.

## Cappuccino –
An equal combination of 1/3 **espresso**, 1/3 hot **steamed milk**, and 1/3 **frothed milk**.

## Classic Cappuccino –
For many, especially the Italians, a cappuccino is a shot of **espresso** with nothing more than **frothed milk** added.

# CAFFÈ LATTE OR CAFÉ AU LAIT?

On the menu boards of espresso bars a caffè latte (pronounced LAH-tay) and a café au lait are most often the same, the former being Italian and the latter French. The French typically drink their morning café au lait in bowls rather than cups, bowls being better than cups for dunking croissants as well as for warming hands.

Lattes are the drinks most often flavored by syrups. Almond and hazelnut are two of the most popular. As with the cappuccino, there are different opinions as to what defines a latte. Remember that taste and versatility are more important than definitions.

## Caffè Latte –

**Espresso** with **steamed milk** added to the cup with little or no foam. Steamed milk or frothed milk are often added to change the strength and proportions of the brew. When more foam is added, the line between a latte and a cappuccino becomes quite vague.

## Caffè Mocha –

Coat the bottom and sides of a cup or mug with approximately 1/4 to 3/4 ounce (a matter of personal preference) of **chocolate syrup**. Add a shot of **espresso**, then fill the cup or mug with **steamed milk** to the point at which you want to add the **whipped cream**. Add whipped cream and dust the top with **grated chocolate, powdered cocoa**, or try some **chocolate chips** to top off the whipped cream. Instead of chocolate syrup, you might want to use **unsweetened cocoa**, adding **sugar** or **vanilla sugar** to taste. Want to try a new twist? Brew with the **whole cloves** as described in the recipe for **Nick's Spiced Americanos** later in this section.

### Latte Macchiato –

A glass or mug of **steamed** and **frothed milk** "marked" by a tablespoon of **espresso** dripped through the foam.

### Espresso Macchiato –

A shot of **espresso** "marked" with a tablespoon of **frothed milk**.

## SOME LESS TRADITIONAL VARIATIONS

### Americano –

A shot of **espresso** to which **hot water** is added, making a full 6 ounce cup. This will be richer and more flavorful than coffee prepared by any other method. Drink it as you would a regular cup of coffee, adding sugar, milk or other flavorings as you like. For even richer flavor, use two shots of **espresso**.

### Breve –

A drink using **half and half** instead of **milk**.

### Viennese Caffè Latte –

A **mocha** with **cinnamon** and an optional dash of **orange flavoring**. Serve with a little freshly grated **orange peel** sprinkled on the **whipped cream**.

### Minted Mocha –

Add a couple of dashes of **mint extract** or crushed **mint leaves** to a **mocha**. Top with **whipped cream** or try adding a dash of mint extract to the cream before whipping for **minted whipped cream**.

### Belgian Breve –

Beat the white of one **egg** until stiff. Add 1/4 teaspoon **vanilla extract** to 1/3 cup **whipping cream**, or flavor with **vanilla sugar**, then beat until stiff. Gently fold the egg white into the whipped cream. Steam the **half and half** for the breve, and pour it into the bottom of a mug. Add the mixture of egg white and whipped cream. Slowly pour either 1 or 2 shots of **espresso** into the mug through the middle of the egg white and whipped cream mixture. Dust with **grated chocolate** if desired.

### Nick's Spiced Americano –

Fill the two-cup filter of your espresso machine halfway with a light dark roast coffee, ground for espresso. Place 5 or 6 **whole cloves** on the grounds. Fill the remainder of the filter with ground espresso, and tamp and brew as you normally would. Add hot water to the **espresso** for a full 8 ounce **Americano**. Twist a zest of **lemon** and **orange** into the Americano before dropping them in the cup. Sweeten to taste.

## COLD ESPRESSO DRINKS

For cold drinks, always use fresh espresso as opposed to that which has been refrigerated. Espresso poured over ice will cool quickly, and the difference in taste will be quite noticeable. If you want to sweeten your cold drink, add sugar to the *hot* espresso before it cools, or use superfine sugar. Regular sugar is nearly impossible to dissolve in a cold drink. For variety, try substituting cooled steamed milk for the cold milk in the following recipes.

### Americano Cubes –

To prevent watering down your drink as the ice melts, try Americano cubes. Brew 4 shots of **espresso** to every quart of water. When cooled to room temperature, pour into ice cube trays for freezing. The flavor of the frozen Americanos seems to stand up to freezing better than that of full strength straight shot espresso and is preferable to melting cubes of plain water in your drink.

### Iced Caffè Latte –

Add 1 or 2 (1 for a short glass, 2 for a tall one) shots of **espresso** to a glass filled with **milk** and **ice** or **Americano cubes**.

### Granita di Caffè –

Heat 2 ounces of **sugar** and a tablespoon of water together in a saucepan until the sugar dissolves. Boil the mixture for a few minutes, then pour three full 8 ounce double **Americanos** into the syrup and add 1 teaspoon of **unsweetened cocoa**. Once the cocoa is dissolved, remove the mixture from the heat and let it cool completely. When cool, pour the mixture into ice cube trays. Freeze. Once completely frozen, place the cubes from one tray in a blender or food processor with 1 cup cold **milk** and blend until slushy. For a smoother granita, add more milk 1/2 cup at a time and blend until the desired consistency is achieved. Spoon the mixture into glasses and serve immediately. For a single serving, blend together 5 or 6 Granita cubes with 1/2 cup milk. Add more milk as necessary.

### Espresso con Ghiaccio e Latte –

Pour one shot of cold **milk** over **ice cubes** and one shot of fresh **espresso** in a short glass or cup.

### Honey Iced Espresso –

Pour equal amounts of fresh **espresso** and **cream** into a short glass or cup filled with **Americano cubes** and drip **honey** to taste.

### Mazagrán Americano –

Brew a 6 ounce **Americano** and sweeten it to taste. Let it cool completely. To the cooled Americano, add a teaspoon of fresh **lemon juice** and 1/2 cup of **club soda**. Pour the mixture in a tall glass of plain **crushed ice**. Garnish with a slice of **lemon**.

### Banana Mocha Cooler –

Pour 8 ounces of **milk** into a blender containing 2 shots of **espresso**, 1 ounce **chocolate syrup**, and a ripe, small-to-medium **banana**. Blend well, then pour in a tall glass filled with **ice** or **Americano cubes**. If too thick to pour, the banana was too large. Either add more milk or spoon it into dessert glasses and call it something else.

## ESPRESSO AND ICE CREAM

### Black and White in Color –

This ice milk dessert keeps well, so you will want to make a little extra. The following is for six servings. Combine 3 cups **whole milk**, 3/4 cup **sugar**, 1 cup **whipping cream**, 2 **cinnamon sticks** and the peel of 1/2 **lemon** in a saucepan. Bring to a boil, stirring constantly. Reduce to a simmer for 30 minutes, stirring occasionally. Remove from heat, remove the lemon peel and cinnamon stick, cool, then refrigerate. To 4 **egg whites**, add 1/2 teaspoon pure **vanilla extract** and 3 drops **lemon juice**, beating until soft peaks are formed. Gradually add 2 tablespoons of **sugar** to the egg white mixture, beating only until stiff.

Slowly and thoroughly beat in the refrigerated mixture. Freeze in shallow baking dishes or pans. Spoon the frozen ice milk into glasses, and add 2 shots **espresso** to each glass, dust with **cinnamon** and serve.

### Espresso Banana Shake –

Add 2 shots **espresso** to a blender containing a medium ripe **banana** and 5 or 6 ounces of **vanilla** or **chocolate ice cream**, a drop of **almond extract**, and 1 tablespoon **sugar**. Blend at high speed until thick and fluffy.

### Vienna Café de Crème –

Brew 2 shots **espresso**. Break a **cinnamon stick** in half and put both halves in the espresso. Let the espresso and cinnamon cool, then refrigerate. Beat 1/2 cup **light cream** with 2/3 cup **vanilla ice cream** until smooth. Stir in 1 tablespoon **brown sugar**. After removing the cinnamon sticks, add the espresso to the mixture and stir well. Pour mixture into a glass, top with **whipped cream** and dust with an equal mixture of **brown sugar**, **cinnamon** and finely **ground coffee**.

### Espresso Float –

Pour 2 tablespoons of **chocolate syrup** over a tall float glass containing 2 scoops of **vanilla** or **chocolate ice cream**, then pour a fresh 8 ounce **Americano** over the syrup and ice cream. If you prefer, the Americano can be cooled before pouring. Top with **whipped cream** and **grated chocolate**.

# SPIRITS AND ESPRESSO

Note: The following recipes that include Americanos will be most enjoyable when the Americano is brewed with the lightest of the dark roasts.

### Espresso Corretto –
Add a few drops of **whiskey**, **brandy**, **Sambuca** or **Cointreau** to a shot of **espresso**.

### Americanos and ? –
Add a half ounce of **Tuaca**, **Sambuca**, **Amaretto** or **brandy** to a freshly brewed Americano. Try topping with a dollop of **whipped cream**.

### Granita di Caffè with Sambuca –
Follow the recipe for **Granita di Caffè** but add 1 ounce **Sambuca** to the boiling **sugar** and **water** mixture about one minute before the mixture is to be removed from the heat. Follow the rest of the recipe as given. For an almond flavor, substitute **Amaretto** for the Sambuca.

### Caffè Kiev –
This recipe is for two servings. Place 1 ounce **semi-sweet chocolate**, 1 rounded teaspoon **sugar** and 1/2 cup of very hot **water** in the top of a double boiler over boiling water. When thoroughly mixed, add 2 tablespoons **cognac**, 2 dashes **vanilla**, 2 tablespoons **crème de cacao**, 1/4 cup **milk** and 1/4 cup **whipping cream** steamed together, and 2 shots **espresso**. Sprinkle freshly grated **nutmeg** in each cup and serve.

### Nick's Spiced Rum Americano –

Rub the inside of a mug with **butter**. Add to the mug 1 ounce **dark rum**, 1 teaspoon **brown sugar**, a **cinnamon stick**, 1 tablespoon of **heavy cream**, 1 strip **orange peel** and some **lemon zest**. Fill the single cup filter of your espresso machine halfway with a light dark roast coffee ground for espresso. Place 5 or 6 **whole cloves** on the grounds. Fill the remainder of the filter with ground espresso, and tamp and brew as you normally would. Pour the shot of **espresso** into the mug, fill with hot water and serve.

### Café Rive Gauche –

Add 3 ounces of **hot chocolate** to 2 shots of **espresso** and mix well. Add 1 ounce **cognac** and a dash of **vanilla** if desired. Top with **whipped cream** and serve.

### An Americano in Paris –

To a 6 ounce **Americano** in a preheated mug, add 1-1/2 tablespoons of **cognac** and gently add 1-1/2 ounces of **whipping cream** and serve.

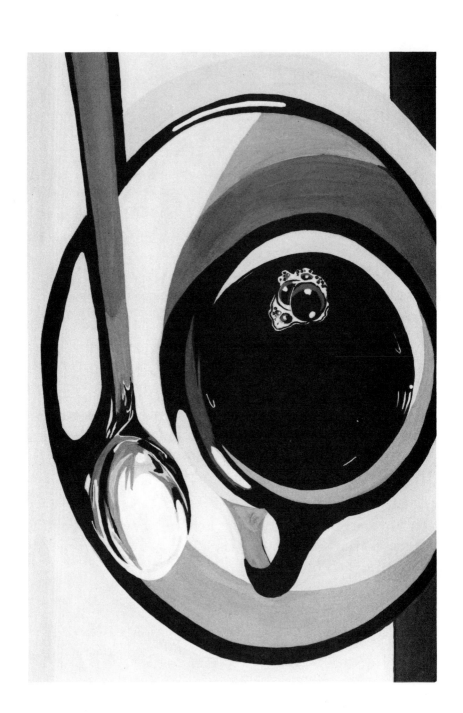

# BREWING
# EXCEPTIONAL COFFEE

*E*SPRESSO IS UNDOUBTEDLY MY FAVORITE WAY TO PRE-
pare and drink coffee. Each cup is fresh and, if
brewed properly, gives the true essence of the
coffee. But it is not the only way I drink coffee. I
also enjoy regularly brewed coffee. Although Americans
drink billions of cups of coffee per year, many people
have never been shown how to make coffee properly.

## GUIDELINES

### Fresh Whole Bean Coffee

As with espresso, start with the freshest possible
whole bean coffee. Your brewed coffee will taste only as
good as the coffee you use.

### The Proper Grind

Grind only as much coffee as you will need for im-
mediate brewing and grind it to the proper consistency for
your coffeemaker. If you use a drip coffeemaker that uses
cone-shaped filters, the grind should be very fine, but not
a powder, and a little coarser than that used for espresso.
If your drip coffeemaker uses a flat-bottomed filter, grind
the coffee a little coarser than that just described. If you
use a French press, or plunger pot, you need to use a
grind that is quite coarse. The longer the brew cycle, the
coarser the grind.

If you use a blade grinder, you can time the grind to give you an adequate idea of what grind you should use. For the cone-shaped filter drip pots, operate the grinder for about 20 to 25 seconds. For those using a flat-bottomed filter, run the grinder for approximately 15 to 20 seconds. For the plunger pot, run the grinder for as little as 6 seconds, and only as long as 9 or 10. Use the times as guidelines, then experiment with the grinds until you find one that works best for you and your coffeemaker.

### Don't Overgrind

The oils and aromatics of the bean can be easily damaged by the heat a grinder produces, especially if a blade grinder is used. Any grinder can break down the bean very quickly, so don't overgrind in the belief that this will yield more flavor or more coffee for the amount of grounds used. Too fine a grind for the coffeemaker will result in a bitter, overextracted cup.

### Use the Correct Amount of Coffee

Use no less than two level tablespoons to a six ounce cup, or two rounded tablespoons for an eight ounce cup. Most people use too little coffee and end up with an overbrewed cup of liquid only vaguely resembling coffee. If the coffee is too strong, add hot water to the pot; don't use less coffee.

### Avoid Overbrewing

By overbrewing, you risk dissolving bitter chemicals out of the grounds and into the cup. If you use an electric filter drip pot, brewing cycles adjust to the amount of water used and not to the amount of coffee. The smaller the amount of coffee, the greater the extraction due to the increased proportion of water to coffee, resulting in overbrewing. As an example, imagine you are going to brew six cups of coffee. If you use two tablespoons per six ounce cup, you will use twelve tablespoons of coffee for the pot, through which you will strain six cups of near boiling water. If you use two level teaspoons per six ounce cup, you will use a total of twelve teaspoons, or four tablespoons of coffee for the pot, and will end up straining the *same* amount of water through one third the coffee – that is overbrewing. The same principle applies to all other regular coffeemakers, from plunger pots to manual or electric drip.

### Use Fresh Water

Coffee gives flavor to water, but it can work the other way around. The alkalinity of hard water affects the essential acids in coffee, giving it a flat taste. Water that has been treated by a water softener can also have a detrimental effect on flavor. The water you use must taste good on its own if you want to make good coffee. If you can't drink your tap water with a smile on your face, you are much better off with bottled or filtered water.

Assuming you are going to use tap water, always use it fresh from the cold tap rather than the hot. Water that has been sitting in a boiler can pick up impurities and unpleasant flavors from the hot water heater as well as the pipes. Some say that cold water contains more oxygen, and is therefore better for brewing. Taste water drawn from the hot tap after it has cooled to room temperature and you will probably agree that water from the cold tap has a much better flavor.

### Do Not Boil

Boiling water poured over coffee will vaporize the aromatics and oils essential to good coffee. The ideal brewing temperature for coffee is between 195°F and

205°F. Water is at the correct temperature for brewing when pea-sized bubbles form. Watch for the bubbles, or wait a minute after boiling, and pour.

### Don't Overheat

One of the advantages espresso has over regularly brewed coffee is its freshness. You drink each cup just after it is made. Coffee that has been sitting on a hot plate or burner becomes bitter and sour in 10 to 20 minutes. Brew only as much as will be consumed in that period of time. Those same aromatics and oils that are damaged by excessive grinding and vaporized by boiling are destroyed by continual heating.

If you have to keep brewed coffee for more than 15 minutes, put the coffee in an insulated pitcher or thermos immediately after brewing. The flavor will last longer. Rinse the container with hot water before filling and the coffee will stay hotter for a longer period of time.

### Filters

For those who like paper filters for the sediment-free cup they brew, look for filters that have been oxygen cleansed. It should be printed on the box. Many filter makers have switched from the chlorine bleach process that produces dioxins harmful to the environment, to the much safer oxygen process that uses considerably less chlorine and poses less of an environmental threat. Unbleached, or "brown bag" filters can impart a distracting taste to coffee if the pulp used for the filters was not sufficiently washed. Worries that resins and other impurities from the unbleached filters might find their way to the pot have prompted many to choose one of the permanent gold-plated metal filters available for almost any drip coffeemaker. The permanent metal filters do not remove essential oils from the coffee and are the most environmentally friendly alternative to paper filters. They cost approximately $20 to $25, a cost quickly offset by the money saved on paper filters.

## A FEW MORE HINTS

Always make sure your brewing equipment is clean. While you shouldn't wash your pot with soap every time you use it, you should scrub it with hot water and occasionally with baking soda to remove the residues that do form. Descaling electric drip pots can be accomplished using a solution of vinegar and water. Coffee loses its flavor long before you need to reheat it. What flavor remains will be lost when the coffee is reheated, so don't put it on your stove, don't microwave it and don't rub it between two sticks. Just pour it down the drain and make fresh coffee. Remove the brew basket with the spent grounds immediately after brewing. Anything that drips through the grounds after brewing has been completed will be bitter. Never reuse coffee grounds after brewing. If you do it once, you will never do it again. Preheat your cup or mug with hot water before filling it with coffee. When cold, the cup can cool coffee very quickly. Never steal a cup before the brewing cycle is complete; doing so will upset the balance of the pot. Unless you use a plunger pot, always stir the finished pot before serving since the coffee that comes out first will be stronger than that which follows. Adding an eggshell to a pot of coffee can clarify the brew, but the calcium in the shell adversely affects the flavor of the coffee by muting its acidity.

## WHICH METHOD IS BEST?

The wonderful thing about coffee is that it can be made well using a number of different methods. There are some ways that are definitely better than others in getting the water to the grounds. The following is a sampling of some of the most popular methods.

## PERCOLATORS

As fond as your memories of the percolator may be, it is best left on the shelf. The sensual gurgle of the percolator is the sound of coffee continually being either boiled or nearly boiled and repeatedly strained through the same grounds until it is considered done, and all at the expense of flavor.

## THE OPEN POT METHOD

The open pot, or "hobo-style" method is the oldest way of making coffee. This method is for those who don't mind a cup with a considerable amount of sediment. Since all you need is a cooking pot, you might want to try this when feeling adventurous or when camping. The recipe below is courtesy of my father.

Use a grind similar to that recommended for a plunger pot, and the proportions of coffee to water given earlier. Heat some water in a pot to a *light* simmer. Put the coffee in the pot and stir only enough to ensure the grounds are completely saturated. Increase the heat until the coffee starts to foam and threaten to run over, stirring it before it actually does. Then lower the heat to the *slightest* simmer for about three to four minutes. Remove from the heat, and sprinkle some cold water over the pot to settle the grounds, or better yet, pour the coffee into the cups through a small mesh strainer.

Though we both now use other brewing methods, some of my fondest coffee memories are of my dad's "hobo-style" brew. Served strong, sweetened with sugar

and condensed milk, in very thick and heavy white ceramic mugs that held about five ounces of coffee, the
memory of that flavor has remained unsurpassed in my
mind.

## *INFUSION*

With the infusion method, near boiling water is
added to a pot containing the grounds. The water and
coffee steep together until the desired strength is reached.
A plunger attached to a fine steel mesh is then pushed to
the bottom of the pot, separating all but the finest grounds
from the coffee. This method is not really much different
than the open pot method, and it produces an excellent
cup with all the flavors of the coffee intact, as long as the
coffee isn't scorched by boiling water. This pot is called a
"plunger pot" or "French press," and is among the most
romantic ways to brew coffee.

The reason for the coarser grind used for the
French press is twofold. With a coarse grind, pushing the
plunger down through the grounds is a simple task. Use
too fine a grind and you will find out just how difficult, if
not impossible, it can become. The surface tension created
by the suspension of finely ground coffee may cause you
to push the plunger down at an angle, and doing so could
result in a broken pot. Water remains in contact with the
grounds during and after steeping. Using too fine a grind
would result in overbrewing, leaving you with a bitter
brew.

Plunger pots can be very inexpensive to very expensive, or anything between. They come in a wide
variety of styles and sizes. Choose the size that best suits
your needs. A friend has two; one for crowds, the other
not. The pots are not insulated, and the coffee can cool

The "French press" or "plunger pot"

somewhat by the time it is through steeping. I believe the cooling is a blessing in disguise. If you want your coffee hot, you must drink it at the optimum time; just after steeping. Timing is crucial; the longer the grounds and coffee are in contact, the more likely it is that the coffee will become bitter.

The French press is perfect for entertaining. Once filled, the attractive pot can be brought to the dinner table to steep.

## DRIP COFFEE

The drip method is the world's most popular way of making coffee. The method is a simple one with a wide assortment of affordable brewers both manual and electric. Rich and full-bodied, drip coffee is made by hot water passing over grounds held in a filter or strainer. Gravity carries the water through the grounds into a waiting container.

Greatest control is offered by manually pouring the water over the grounds. A drawback to the method is the cooling that can occur before the coffee is ready to serve. There are several ways to avoid using an outside heat source to keep your coffee hot. The best by far is to use one of the filter holders that let you brew directly into an attached thermos or other insulated container. Preheating is simple and advisable; rinse the container with hot water just before brewing.

After you have poured some water over the grounds, stir them to make sure they are completely saturated. By stirring the grounds you break up any lumps that may have formed as well eliminate any fissures the water could use as a quick path to the pot, bypassing the grounds.

## NEAPOLITAN FLIP-POT

The neapolitan flip-pots are charming, and deserve mention for that reason as well as the fact that they make great coffee. Unfortunately, they are becoming increasingly difficult to find.

This design holds the coffee in a strainer between two pots that are screwed or clamped together. Water is heated in the lower pot, and when it is hot enough, the whole combination is flipped over. The water that was below the coffee, is now above it, until it can drip through the grounds into the pot that used to be on top, but is now on the bottom.

You need to use a heat dissipating pad to prevent overheating the coffee while brewing. Not boiling the water before brewing can be a little tricky, but the flip-pot is a coffeemaker that makes up in charm what it lacks in technology. A word of caution with the flip-pot. Make sure everything is screwed or clamped tightly together to prevent the possibility of burning or having coffee leak all over your stove.

## ELECTRIC DRIP POTS

Most compatible with the harried lifestyle of a great many coffee drinkers is the automatic electric filter drip coffeemaker. Fill it with water, add coffee, flip a switch, and come back minutes later to a pot of fresh coffee.

It was a tidal wave of "Mr. Coffees" that drove the percolator out of the American kitchen into deserved obscurity. The first electric drip machines were superior to the percolator, but still left a lot to be desired. The refinements since their introduction in the early Seventies has improved their performance immeasurably. The new-est machines are so feature-laden that purchasing one can be more complicated than buying stereo equipment. Consult a consumer guide before making your choice.

## SUMMARY

Coffee, such an enjoyable diversion, such an accessible luxury, deserves the time it takes to develop your own style of preparing and serving this delightful beverage.

And mom, sorry about bashing the percolator.

# DESSERTS

*E*SPRESSO IS A BEVERAGE BOTH INTENSE AND SUBTLE, often served without accompaniment. Many foods could be overpowered by the flavor of espresso and its variations. Others could dominate the complex flavor of espresso. Foods served with espresso should complement rather than compete. Those most complementary are desserts. The following recipes are for a variety of desserts that will help enhance your enjoyment of espresso.

Many of the recipes call for **vanilla sugar.** To make vanilla sugar, put one or two vanilla pods in a quart-sized jar. Fill the jar with sugar and cover tightly. In a few days, the sugar will have been flavored by the vanilla and can then be used in place of plain sugar. Replenish the sugar as you use it. A vanilla pod will last many months in a tightly closed container.

Note: Recipes calling for butter and eggs can be enjoyed by those who need to limit their intake of cholesterol. Simply substitute margarine for butter and egg substitutes for egg yolks. Egg whites contain no cholesterol and must be used in the recipes calling for beaten egg whites.

# COOKIES

## BISCOTTI

*Makes 12 to 18*

2-1/4 cups all-purpose flour
3/4 cup superfine sugar
1-1/2 teaspoons baking powder
2 eggs
1 egg yolk
Pinch of salt
2/3 cup chopped almonds
1 egg white plus 2 tablespoons milk for glazing

Preheat oven to 425°F. Lightly grease and flour a baking sheet. Mix the first six ingredients together, blending until smooth. Knead the almonds into the dough until evenly distributed. Divide the dough into halves and form each half into a flattened cigar shape. Brush each log with the egg-milk glaze. Place on the baking sheet, leaving at least 3 inches between each log. Bake at 425°F for 10 minutes; brush with glaze once again and continue to bake for another 10 to 12 minutes, or just until golden. Brush with glaze once more. Cool until just warm to the touch, then slice into 1 inch slices. Lay slices on baking sheets, no edges touching, and bake for 5 minutes more. Remove and cool completely on a wire rack before serving or storing. For a more festive touch, dip in melted semisweet chocolate.

## SERBIAN POPPY SEED COOKIES

*Makes 18 to 24*

8 ounces cream cheese, room temperature
8 ounces butter (2 sticks), at room temperature
1 cup vanilla sugar (see page 135)
1 teaspoon lemon juice
2-3/4 cups all-purpose flour
1 can (12-1/2 oz.) poppy seed filling
1/4 cup finely ground almonds

Beat together cream cheese, butter, sugar, and lemon juice. Add the flour gradually until thoroughly blended. Divide the dough into quarters, wrap and chill until firm to the touch, not hard, at least 2 hours. Meanwhile, beat the poppy seed filling and almonds for 1 minute. Preheat oven to 350°F. Working on one quarter at a time, roll out dough between two sheets of waxed paper to no more than 1/8 inch thick. Cut out 3 inch circles using the top of a drinking glass or a cookie cutter. Place half the circles on a baking sheet. Put a rounded tablespoon of poppy seed filling on the center of each one. Cover each with the other half of the circles; press the edges together to seal. With shears or sharp knife, cut an "X" design in the top of each cookie. Chill and re-roll dough scraps until all dough is used. Bake 18 to 12 minutes until golden around the edges. Cool on wire rack.

## CHOCOLATE HAZELNUT LOGS

*Makes 36*

1-1/2 cups vanilla sugar (see page 135)
1 cup finely ground hazelnuts
2 eggs
1-1/2 tablespoons freshly brewed espresso
1-3/4 cups all-purpose flour
2 ounces melted butter (1/2 stick)
1/2 cup semisweet chocolate

Preheat oven to 350°F. Mix sugar, hazelnuts, eggs and espresso until thoroughly blended. Add flour, mix well. Stir in melted butter. Using a tablespoon, scoop a small amount of dough and roll into a little log. Repeat until dough is used up. Bake on lightly greased baking sheets in a 350°F oven. Cool on wire rack. Meanwhile, melt the chocolate in a double boiler. Dip one end of the logs into the melted chocolate and stand them up on a wire rack just long enough to allow the chocolate to set.

## ESPRESSO CHOCOLATE CHIP SQUARES

*Makes 36*

*Crust:*

2 cups all-purpose flour
1/2 cup powdered sugar
Pinch of salt
8 ounces butter (2 sticks), cold, cut into 1/4 inch pieces
1-1/2 teaspoons vanilla extract

Preheat oven to 350°F. Place all ingredients in mixer bowl or food processor. Beat or process until dough forms a ball. Press out evenly in a 13 x 9 inch cake pan. Bake in a 350°F oven 20 to 25 minutes, until the edges just start to turn golden. Put on wire rack to cool. Keep oven at 350°F.

*Topping:*

4 ounces butter (1 stick) at room temperature
3/4 cup packed light brown sugar
2 large eggs
1/4 cup milk
1 teaspoon vanilla extract
1 cup all-purpose flour
2 tablespoons finely ground espresso coffee
2 tablespoons unsweetened cocoa powder
Pinch of salt
1 cup semisweet chocolate chips

Beat butter and sugar together until fluffy. Add all other ingredients except chocolate chips. Mix just until blended. Add chips, stirring by hand. Pour mixture over the cooled crust, spreading evenly with spatula. Bake about 20 to 25 minutes, until the topping sets. Cool completely on wire rack, then cut into 36 squares.

*A variation:*

Spread strawberry, raspberry or blackberry jam over cooled crust. Cut into 36 squares. Top each square with fresh berries of the same type as the preserve you use.

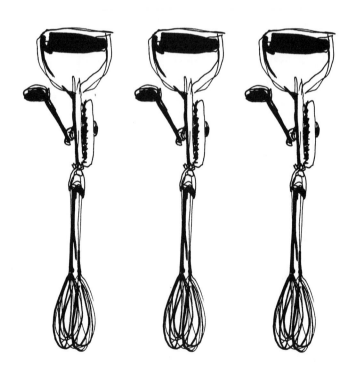

# A COOKIE LOVER'S CHOCOLATE CHIP COOKIE

*Makes about 30 cookies*

4 ounces butter (1 stick)
1/2 cup brown sugar, packed
1/2 cup sugar
1/2 teaspoon vanilla extract
1 egg
1 cup flour
3/4 cup oatmeal, processed until a fine powder
Dash of salt
1/2 teaspoon baking soda
1/2 teaspoon baking powder
3/4 cup walnuts (or any nut you prefer)
1 cup semisweet chocolate chips

Preheat oven to 350°F. Cream together butter, brown sugar and sugar. Add vanilla and egg; stir well. Mix together the flour, oatmeal, salt, baking soda and baking powder and add to the butter mixture, blending thoroughly. Stir in the nuts and chocolate chips. Refrigerate the dough for at least one half hour. This dough stores very well in the refrigerator or the freezer so it can be made ahead and used as needed. Shape into 1 inch balls and place 2 inches apart on baking sheet. Bake in a 350°F oven for 8 to 12 minutes, until the edges are turning golden.

## ALMOND CRESCENTS

*Makes 48*

2 egg yolks
8 ounces butter (2 sticks), at room temperature
1/2 cup vanilla sugar (see page 135)
1 teaspoon almond extract
1 cup finely ground blanched almonds
2-2/3 cups sifted all-purpose flour
1 cup vanilla sugar

Beat together the butter, yolks, sugar and almond extract until creamy. Add almonds and half the flour. Blend just until combined, then stir in the remaining half by hand. Divide the dough into 4 equal portions. Wrap and refrigerate at least 1 hour or overnight. Preheat oven to 375°F. Form each quarter into a 12 inch rope, then cut each rope into 12 one inch pieces. Form these into 3 inch logs, tapering each end to a point, then place one inch apart on baking sheets, forming each into a crescent shape. Bake 12 to 15 minutes. Cool on wire rack until cool enough to handle. Gently roll each crescent in the vanilla sugar to coat. Replace on rack to complete cooling.

## BANANA PUFFS

*Makes 42 cookies*

8 ounces butter (2 sticks), at room temperature
1 cup brown sugar, packed
2 eggs
8 ounces mashed, very ripe bananas (2 medium)
1/2 cup buttermilk
1 teaspoon vanilla extract
3 cups all-purpose flour
1-1/2 teaspoons baking soda
Pinch of salt
1 cup sliced almonds

Beat together the butter, sugar and eggs until creamy. Stir in the bananas, buttermilk and vanilla, blending well. Sift together flour, soda and salt. Stir into butter mixture, forming a smooth dough. Blend in nuts. Wrap and chill dough for one hour. Preheat oven to 375°F. Drop the dough by the teaspoonful onto greased baking sheets, no closer than 2 inches apart. Bake at 375°F for 10 minutes, just until edges turn golden.

## ORANGE ALMOND CURLS

*Makes 24*

1/3 cup all-purpose flour
2/3 cup powdered sugar
1 teaspoon vanilla extract
2 tablespoons orange-flavored liqueur
1 teaspoon almond extract
2 egg whites, lightly beaten
Grated zest (colored part of peel) of two oranges
1 cup blanched almonds, sliced
4 ounces butter (1 stick), at room temperature

Preheat oven to 400°F. Mix the flour and sugar together until well blended. Add vanilla, orange liqueur, grated zest, almond extract, eggs and almonds, stirring until thoroughly mixed. Beat the butter in until the dough has a smooth consistency. Lightly grease baking sheets. Drop the dough by the teaspoonful onto the prepared sheets, leaving very generous space between each drop, putting no more than six per sheet. Bake in 400°F oven for 6 to 8 minutes. Remove cookies from sheets and immediately drape over a rolling pin or other similar cylindrical object. Allow to cool so the shape will set. Carefully remove (best way is to gently slide the cookies sideways) and arrange on serving tray or store in airtight container.

## LEMON ALMOND COOKIES

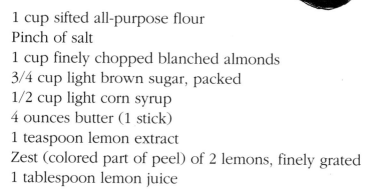

*Makes 36*

1 cup sifted all-purpose flour
Pinch of salt
1 cup finely chopped blanched almonds
3/4 cup light brown sugar, packed
1/2 cup light corn syrup
4 ounces butter (1 stick)
1 teaspoon lemon extract
Zest (colored part of peel) of 2 lemons, finely grated
1 tablespoon lemon juice

Thoroughly blend the first three ingredients. Set aside. Preheat oven to 350°F. Grease two baking sheets. In a saucepan, combine the next three ingredients and bring to a boil, stirring frequently. Remove from heat and stir in the flour mixture as well as the lemon extract, zest, and juice. Blend thoroughly until the batter is smooth.

Drop the batter by the half-teaspoonful onto the greased baking sheets. Bake just until golden around the edges, about 9 to 10 minutes. Cool slightly on sheets; transfer to wire racks to complete cooling.

# TILE WAFERS

*Makes 36*

1 egg white
1/4 cup sugar
Pinch of salt
1/4 teaspoon vanilla extract
1 teaspoon almond extract
1 teaspoon brandy or cognac
4 tablespoons flour
2 tablespoons melted butter
3 tablespoons finely chopped almonds
3 tablespoons sliced almonds

Preheat oven to 375°F. Beat together egg white, salt, vanilla extract, almond extract and brandy or cognac until frothy. Gradually add flour while beating until smooth. Add melted butter. Stir well. Add chopped almonds, stirring until well blended. The batter should be thin. Add a little more brandy if necessary. Drop a teaspoon of batter for each cookie onto well greased baking sheets, spreading each drop to a diameter of 1-1/2 inches. Sprinkle each with a few of the sliced almonds. Bake 4 to 5 minutes, until a pale golden color. Have waiting 2 dowel rods or wooden spoon handles placed across a tray or plate. When you remove the cookies from the oven, be prepared to work quickly. Gently lift the cookies with a spatula and place each one over the dowels or spoon handles, applying gentle pressure to the edges as they curve downward. In case your cookies are too cool to bend, return them to the oven for a few seconds and try again. After they are properly curved, cool before removing to serving tray.

## VIENNESE PASTRY COOKIES

*Makes 36*

8 ounces cream cheese at room temperature
8 ounces butter (2 sticks), at room temperature
2-1/2 cups all-purpose flour
Fruit preserves, commercial or homemade

Cream together the cream cheese, and butter with an electric mixer or in a food processor. Gradually add the flour until a smooth dough forms. Gently knead by hand for a few minutes; wrap and refrigerate 12 hours or overnight. Preheat oven to 375°F. Roll out to about 1/2 inch thickness. Cut into squares, make a well in the center with thumb or the back of a teaspoon. Place a dab of fruit preserves such as raspberry, strawberry, blackberry, etc. in the well. Bake at 375°F for about 20 minutes, until edges are golden. When completely cooled, sprinkle with powdered sugar.

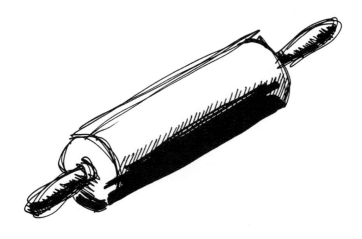

## SUGAR COOKIES

*Makes about 48 cookies*

8 ounces butter (2 sticks), at room temperature
1 egg yolk
1 tablespoon powdered sugar
1 tablespoon brandy or cognac
2 cups all-purpose flour
1/2 teaspoon cinnamon
About 2 cups sifted powdered sugar for dusting

Preheat oven to 300°F. Beat the butter until creamy. Mix the egg yolk, sugar and brandy together in another bowl, then beat into the butter. Gradually mix the flour into the butter mixture. The dough will be slightly sticky. Flour your hands and form the dough into balls about 1 inch in diameter. Place on baking sheet about 2 inches apart. Bake at 300°F for 30 minutes; do not allow to brown. Cool for 3 minutes. Roll the cookies in the powdered sugar, coating on all sides. After the cookies are completely cooled, dust them again with powdered sugar.

# CAKES AND DESSERT BREADS

## ESPRESSO CHOCOLATE CAKE

*Serves 8*

8 ounces butter (2 sticks), at room temperature
1/2 cup semisweet chocolate chips
1-3/4 cups light brown sugar
3 eggs
1 tablespoon vanilla extract
1/4 cup espresso, freshly brewed, room temperature
3/4 cup milk
1-1/2 cups all-purpose flour
1/2 teaspoon baking soda
1/2 teaspoon baking powder

Preheat oven to 350°F. Butter a large tube or bundt pan. Cut parchment paper to fit bottom, butter the paper and then flour the bottom and sides of the pan and the paper. Melt chocolate chips in the top of a double boiler over briskly simmering water. Set aside. Cream together the butter and brown sugar until fluffy. Add eggs one at a time, stirring between each, then add vanilla. Stir. Mix espresso and milk. Sift together flour, baking soda and baking powder in a separate bowl. Add espresso mixture to butter mixture, blending thoroughly. Next add flour mixture gradually while beating, blending thoroughly. Pour batter into pan. Bake at 350°F for about 60 minutes, or until a toothpick inserted in the center comes out clean. Cool on wire rack. Invert onto plate when completely cool. Serve plain or with raspberries and whipped cream.

## BANANA NUT BREAD

*Serves 8*

6 ounces butter (1-1/2 sticks), at room temperature
1-1/3 cups sugar
2 extra large eggs or 3 medium (1/2 cup),
  at room temperature
3 cups all-purpose flour
4 teaspoons baking powder
1/3 cup milk, at room temperature
3/4 cups chopped walnuts or pecans
1-1/2 cups ripe mashed bananas (3 medium)

Preheat oven to 350°F. Beat butter for 2 minutes. Gradually add sugar while continuing to beat for at least another minute after the sugar is added. One at a time, beat in the eggs, continuing to beat for 2 minutes, or until the mixture is very fluffy. Sift the flour and baking powder together. Add flour to butter mixture one cup at a time, beating about a minute after each addition. Add milk, then the nuts, beating continuously. Beat in the mashed bananas. The batter should be smooth and silky. Pour it into a well greased 13 x 4-1/2 x 2-1/2 inch loaf pan. Bake at 350°F for about 1 hour and 10 minutes, or until a toothpick inserted in the center comes out clean. Cool on a wire rack for about 15 minutes, then gently loosen the sides with a knife and invert onto a serving plate.

## HAZELNUT CAKE

*Serves 12*

1 cup hazelnuts
1 cup cornmeal
8 ounces butter (2 sticks), at room temperature
1 cup sugar
1 teaspoon almond extract
4 large eggs, separated
1 cup all-purpose flour
1 pint fresh raspberries (frozen is ok if fresh
   not available)

Preheat oven to 350°F. Butter a 9 inch tube or bundt pan. Toast nuts on baking sheet until browned, about 15 minutes. Cool. Rub the roasted nuts in a towel to loosen and remove as much skin as possible. Process nuts and cornmeal in food processor or food grinder until very fine. Beat butter, sugar, salt and almond extract until fluffy. Add yolks, blending thoroughly. Add nut mixture; stir in flour gently by hand. Beat egg whites until stiff peaks form. Gently fold 1/3 of the egg whites into the batter, then fold in remaining egg whites until well blended. Pour batter into prepared pan. Bake about 1 hour, or until a toothpick inserted in the center comes out clean. Cool on wire rack. When completely cool, invert cake onto serving platter. Slice and serve with raspberries or other fruit of your choice.

## POPPY SEED LEMON CAKE

*Serves 8*

2/3 cup poppy seeds
2/3 cup milk plus 1/4 cup milk
6 ounces butter (1-1/2 sticks),
    at room temperature
1-1/4 cup vanilla sugar (see page 135)
2 cups sifted cake flour
2 teaspoons baking powder
Pinch of salt
2 tablespoons lemon zest
Powdered sugar for dusting

Soak poppy seeds in 2/3 cup milk for 2 hours. Preheat the oven to 400°F. Beat together the butter and sugar until creamy. Sift together flour, baking powder and salt, and set aside. Combine the soaked poppy seed mixture with the 1/4 cup milk and the lemon zest. Add half the flour and half the poppy seed mixture to the butter-sugar mixture, blending thoroughly. Add the rest and repeat. Choose two 9 x 9 inch cake pans, or one 4-1/2 x 8 inch loaf pan or one large tube pan, depending on how you want the cake to look. Prepare the pans by lining with parchment paper or greasing and flouring the bottom and sides. Bake in 400°F oven for 55 to 65 minutes if using a loaf pan, 35 to 45 minutes in tube pan or in square pans. Cool on wire rack. Dust with powdered sugar.

## ESPRESSO AMARETTO CAKE

*Serves 12*

1-1/2 cups sliced almonds
8 ounces butter (2 sticks), at room temperature
2 cups sugar
1 tablespoon finely ground espresso coffee
2 cups all-purpose flour
1 tablespoon freshly brewed espresso, cooled
1 teaspoon vanilla extract
1/2 teaspoon almond extract

Preheat oven to 350°F. Lightly toast almonds by spreading evenly on a baking sheet and placing in oven for 8 to 10 minutes. Do not allow almonds to brown. Remove when just golden and set aside. Grease a 10 inch bundt pan or a 4-1/2 x 8 inch loaf pan. Sprinkle 1/2 cup of the toasted almonds uniformly over the bottom of the pan. Cream together the butter, sugar and ground espresso until fluffy. Add the flour, stirring only until blended. Add espresso liquid and the vanilla and almond extracts; stir. Add eggs one at a time, stirring after each one. Gently fold in the remaining almonds. Pour batter into the pan and bake at 350°F for about 70 minutes or until a toothpick inserted in the center comes out clean. About halfway through baking time, cover the pan tightly with aluminum foil.

While cake is baking, prepare the syrup:

6 tablespoons sugar
6 tablespoons Amaretto liqueur
1 tablespoon freshly brewed espresso

Slowly heat all three ingredients in a saucepan, stirring constantly until the sugar melts. Set aside.

Remove cake from oven when done. Poke holes all over the top of the cake. Carefully spoon on half the syrup until it is absorbed into the holes. Cool the cake in its pan on a wire rack for 10 minutes. Invert cake onto plate by placing plate upside down on top of pan; grasp plate and pan securely and turn over. Remove pan. Poke holes all over the top and side of the cake. Spoon or brush remaining syrup over cake and allow to cool completely before serving. Amount of liqueur can be increased according to your own preference.

# PASTRIES AND TARTS

## BOMBOLONI

*Makes 48*

1 ounce fresh yeast or 1 packet dry yeast
3/4 cup warm milk
2-1/2 cups all-purpose flour, sifted
2 eggs
2 ounces butter (1/2 stick), at room temperature
1/4 cup sugar
Pinch of salt
Oil for deep frying
Powdered sugar or regular sugar for dusting

Dissolve the yeast in the milk. Let stand for about 5 minutes. Put the flour in a bowl and make a well in the center. Pour in the yeast mixture and mix well. Stir in the eggs, butter, sugar, and salt. Beat until thoroughly mixed and a smooth dough forms. Do not overbeat. Knead the dough on a floured surface until elastic, about 5 minutes. Cover the dough and let rise in a warm, draft-free place until doubled in size. Punch down and knead for 10 minutes. Form the dough into a ball, place on a baking sheet, cover with a clean, damp cloth and let rise in a warm place for 5 to 6 hours. Knead the dough on a floured surface for 10 minutes. Form the dough into a ball, cover and refrigerate for at least 5 hours or overnight for a superior dough. Roll out on a floured board to about 1 inch in thickness. Cut out 2 inch circles; shape into balls. Have the oil preheated to 370°F, and at least 3 inches deep. Fry just a few at a time, until golden; turn over with slotted spoon and fry until golden on all sides. Carefully remove with slotted spoon or frying basket, and drain well on paper towels. Sift the powdered sugar over the bomboloni, or if you prefer, roll them in regular sugar or a sugar-cinnamon mixture.

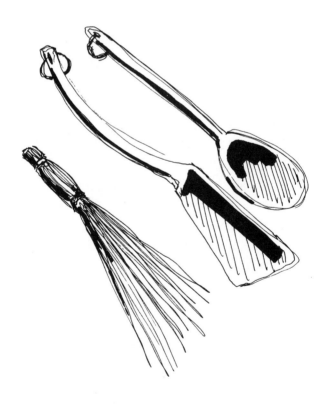

## ESPRESSO NUT SCONES

*Makes 14*

1 cup toasted hazelnuts, chopped
1 cup milk
2 teaspoons espresso, finely ground
2-1/2 cups all-purpose flour
1 tablespoon baking powder
Pinch of salt
4 ounces butter (1 stick), at room temperature
2/3 cup packed brown sugar

Toast the hazelnuts in a preheated 350°F oven for 15 minutes. Put the nuts in a towel and rub briskly to loosen and remove the skins. Chop the cleaned nuts by hand or use a food processor. Combine the milk and espresso; set aside. Sift together flour, baking powder and salt. Add butter, and, with a pastry blender or electric mixer, cut in until the mixture forms granules similar in texture to cornmeal. Add the hazelnuts and brown sugar to the flour and mix thoroughly. Add milk mixture and stir well. Scoop dough by quarter cupfuls and drop onto an ungreased baking sheet. Bake in a preheated 400°F oven for 12 to 15 minutes, just until golden.

## NEW ORLEANS BEIGNETS

*Makes 24*

3 tablespoons freshly brewed espresso
3 tablespoons water
1 tablespoon butter
6 tablespoons all-purpose flour
4 eggs
1 teaspoon vanilla extract
1 teaspoon lemon juice
Vegetable oil for frying

Preheat oil for deep frying to 375°F. Combine espresso, water, butter, and flour in a saucepan. Bring to a boil, stirring continuously. Lower heat, continue to cook and stir for 5 minutes. Remove from heat. Beat in the eggs one at a time, and after the last egg is added, beat for another 4 minutes. Add the vanilla and lemon juice and beat for 1 minute more. Drop the batter by the teaspoonful into the hot oil, being careful to avoid splashing the oil. Cook until golden. Remove with slotted spoon or frying basket. Drain on paper towels. Dust with powdered sugar or roll in vanilla sugar (see page 135) if desired.

# CHEESECAKE TARTS

*Makes 15*

4 ounces butter (1 stick), at room temperature
1/4 cup sugar
1 egg
1 teaspoon grated lemon rind
1-1/2 cups all-purpose flour, sifted
8 ounces softened cream cheese
1/2 cup sugar
1/2 teaspoon vanilla extract
2 eggs
1-1/2 teaspoon lemon juice
1/4 cup sour cream
2 cups fresh or frozen berries or sliced fresh fruit, assorted
1/2 cup warmed strawberry jelly

Beat together butter and sugar for 2 minutes. Add lemon rind and egg. Mix well. Stir in flour, blend well to form a smooth dough. Refrigerate at least 1 hour. Preheat oven to 400°F. Roll out dough on floured surface. Cut out 15 three-inch circles. Line small pastry tins or individual muffin pan cups with dough. Lightly pierce dough on bottom and sides with a fork. Bake in 400°F oven for 10 minutes until the crust turns golden. Put aside. Beat cream cheese until smooth, then add sugar, vanilla, eggs, lemon juice and sour cream, and beat for 2 minutes longer. Pour this mixture into the baked shells, filling each to within 1/2 inch of the top. Bake in 400°F oven for 10 minutes. Cool. Loosen the edges of the pastry with a small, sharp knife for easier removal. Place tarts on tray; cover and chill. Just before serving, arrange berries or fruit on top of each tart. Brush with warm jelly to glaze.

## ELEPHANT EARS

*Makes 24*

1 sheet (8 ounces) frozen puff pastry
1/2 cup sugar
1 teaspoon grated lemon zest
1 tablespoon cinnamon

Thaw pastry according to directions. Line baking sheets with parchment paper or grease well and flour. Sprinkle 1/4 cup sugar over the work surface. Put the puff pastry on the sugar. With rolling pin, roll out to 1/8 inch thickness. Trim with a very sharp knife to exactly 10 x 12 inches. Combine the remaining 1/4 cup sugar, lemon zest and cinnamon. Sprinkle 2 tablespoons of the mixture evenly over the pastry. Fold the 10 inch sides of the rectangle to the middle so they nearly touch. Press by rolling a rolling pin over the folded pastry. Sprinkle with 1 tablespoon of the sugar mixture. Fold the 10 inch sides once again so they nearly touch in the middle, and lightly press with the rolling pin. Sprinkle with remaining sugar mixture, and fold as before once more. Wrap tightly and place in the freezer until firm, about 20 minutes. Meanwhile, preheat oven to 400°F. With a very sharp knife, slice the pastry into 3/8 inch slices. Gently lift the slices with a spatula and place on baking sheets at least 2 inches apart. Bake 10 minutes; turn over, baking until crisp and sugar caramelizes, about 3 to 5 minutes more. Watch carefully during this stage to prevent burning. Place on wire rack to cool.

## PECAN TARTS

*Makes 20*

4 ounces cream cheese at room temperature
4 ounces butter (1 stick), at room temperature
1 cup all-purpose flour
1 large egg
1 cup brown sugar, well-packed
1/2 tablespoon melted butter
1 teaspoon vanilla extract
1 teaspoon lemon juice
1 cup chopped pecans

Beat together cream cheese and butter until thoroughly blended. Gradually add flour, stirring until the dough is smooth. Form the dough into a ball, wrap, and chill for at least 1 hour. Meanwhile, beat the eggs lightly, then add the sugar, melted butter, vanilla, lemon juice, stirring well. Mix in pecans. Preheat oven to 350°F. Use miniature muffin pans or tiny tart pans. Take a piece of dough slightly larger than a walnut, line a muffin cup or tart pan by pressing the dough evenly across the bottom and up the sides. Repeat until dough is used up. Fill each shell with the pecan mixture to within 1/4 inch of the top. Bake in 350°F oven for 25 to 28 minutes, or just until the crust turns golden brown. Cool for at least five minutes. Loosen each shell carefully. Remove from pans and complete cooling on wire rack.

## ALMOND TWISTS

*Makes 18*

1 10 inch sheet frozen puff pastry
1 egg, slightly beaten
4 tablespoons sugar
1/2 cup sliced almonds, lightly toasted and chopped

Thaw puff pastry according to directions. Preheat oven to 400°F. Unroll to a 10 inch square; adjust with rolling pin if necessary. Brush one side with egg, then sprinkle with 2 tablespoons sugar and 1/4 cup almonds. Turn the pastry over and repeat, using up the remaining ingredients. Cut the dough in half, then cut each half into strips 1" x 5" long. Hold one end of a strip and twist, laying twisted strip on a slightly dampened baking sheet, pressing the ends down to prevent the dough from un-twisting. Repeat with each strip. Bake in 400°F oven for 10 minutes. Cool on wire racks. Will not keep for more than two days.

# PUDDINGS, CREAMS AND A MOUSSE

## RICOTTA AL CAFFÈ

*Makes 4 servings*

3/4 cup ricotta cheese, fresh if possible
3 tablespoons superfine sugar
1 tablespoon espresso, finely ground
4 tablespoons Amaretto liqueur
4 tablespoons freshly brewed espresso, at room
    temperature

Mix all the ingredients together, using an electric mixer, or process in a blender until smooth and creamy.

In Italy, some variations include:

Add 1/2 cup of diced seasonal fruit after the other ingredients are blended, mix well.

Add 1/4 cup shaved chocolate, or 1/4 cup un-sweetened cocoa if a less sweet flavor is desired.

Add 2 stiffly beaten egg whites, folding them gently into the mixture to create a fluffier, lighter version.

## BUDINO di RICOTTA
## (RICOTTA PUDDING)

*Serves 6*

2 eggs, separated
1/2 cup superfine sugar
2 ounces freshly brewed espresso, at room temperature
2 tablespoons very finely ground espresso
2 lbs. ricotta cheese, fresh if possible
1/2 cup cream, whipped to soft peaks
2 tablespoons unsweetened cocoa powder

Beat together the egg yolks, half the sugar, and the espresso, both liquid and ground. Add the ricotta, blending thoroughly. Beat the egg whites until soft peaks form, while gradually adding the other half of the sugar. Gently fold the whipped cream into the ricotta mixture; repeat with egg white mixture. Pour into a wet mold 6 to 8 inches in diameter (a classic fluted mold is traditional), and refrigerate for at least 4 hours. To unmold, place the mold in warm water for a few seconds, place serving plate upside down on the top of the mold, turn over and carefully lift mold away. Garnish the pudding with the cocoa provided, or with cinnamon if you prefer.

## TUSCAN TRIFLE or TIRAMISU

*Serves 6*

3 egg yolks
3 tablespoons superfine sugar
1-1/3 cup Marsala wine or good quality brandy
1/4 cup freshly brewed espresso
8 ounces Mascarpone cheese, at room temperature
1/2 cup whipping cream
1 egg white
4 ounces lady fingers

Beat the egg yolks and sugar in the top of a double boiler over gently simmering water until frothy. Add 1/3 of the wine or brandy, beating constantly until the mixture begins to thicken. Cool. Blend the espresso and cheese together. Whip the cream to soft peaks. Beat the egg white until stiff peaks form. Gently fold the egg white into the egg yolk mixture. Dip the lady fingers into the remaining wine or brandy, and arrange them in a single layer in the bottom of a 9 inch bowl. Cover with half the Mascarpone cheese and espresso mixture, then half the egg yolk mixture, then half the cream. Repeat the layers, finishing with the cream. Chill for at least 2 hours before serving.

NOTE: 8 ounces ricotta, 1 ounce cream cheese and 1 teaspoon lemon juice processed in a blender or food processor can be substituted for the Mascarpone cheese.

## ESPRESSO ZABAGLIONE

*Makes 4 servings*

3 fresh eggs, separated
1/4 cup Marsala wine or very good brandy
1/3 cup freshly brewed espresso
3 tablespoons superfine sugar

Combine the egg yolks, wine and espresso and beat until thoroughly blended. Beat the egg whites and sugar until the mixture forms stiff peaks. Gently fold the egg white mixture into the egg yolk mixture. Serve by itself or:

Pour over slices of pound cake; garnish with fresh fruit or berries.

Line dessert bowls with crushed Amaretto cookies; pour in zabaglione; garnish with shaved chocolate.

Fill fresh ripe peach halves with the zabaglione; sprinkle with cinnamon and nutmeg.

Zabaglione may be frozen, so it is an excellent make-ahead sauce or dessert for entertaining.

## MOCHA CHOCOLATE MOUSSE

*Makes 12 servings*

1 pound semisweet chocolate, broken
4 ounces butter (1 stick), at room temperature
2 ounces freshly brewed espresso
2 ounces water
2 egg yolks
1/4 cup coffee liqueur
4 egg whites
4 tablespoons sugar
1 cup heavy cream

Combine chocolate, butter, espresso and water in the top half of a double boiler over actively simmering water, stirring constantly until the chocolate is melted and the mixture is smooth and silky. Beat the yolks slightly; add liqueur. Stir in a small amount of the hot chocolate mixture, then stir the entire yolk mixture into the rest of the chocolate mixture. Cool to room temperature. Meanwhile, beat egg whites in a large bowl just until soft peaks form. Gradually beat in the 4 tablespoons of sugar until stiff peaks form. Spoon over the chocolate mixture. Fold very gently. Beat the cream until stiff peaks form; gently fold into the chocolate and egg white mixture. Chill thoroughly, at least 4 hours.

## BAVARIAN MOCHA CREAM

*Serves 6*

1/4 cup whole espresso coffee beans
1/2 cup milk
2 tablespoons cold water
1 tablespoon unflavored gelatin
1/4 cup sugar
4 egg yolks
1 teaspoon vanilla extract
2 cups whipping cream

Bring the milk to a boil. Remove from heat. Immediately add espresso beans. Set aside, allowing to cool to room temperature. Meanwhile, soak the gelatin in the water. Strain the cooled milk to remove the coffee beans. In the top of a double boiler, beat together the sugar, egg yolks and vanilla. The water in the bottom pan of the double boiler should be at a gentle simmer. Pour a small amount of the milk into the egg mixture; stirring constantly, slowly add the rest of the milk. Stir in the gelatin, stir and cook until completely dissolved. Remove from heat. Chill until the mixture begins to set. Whip the cream until stiff peaks form. Fold the cream gently into the other ingredients. When well blended, place the mixture into the bowl from which you intend to serve it, or into a mold. Melon shaped molds are classic for Bavarian Creams. To make unmolding easier, wet the mold before filling. Chill at least 12 hours if using a mold, 4 hours if using individual dessert dishes. To unmold, place mold in warm water for 10 to 15 seconds, place plate on top of mold and invert. Garnish plate with shaved chocolate or piped whipped cream if desired.

# ICE CREAM AND CANDY

## ESPRESSO GELATO

*Serves 6*

4 egg yolks
1/2 cup superfine sugar
1 teaspoon almond extract
1 cup freshly brewed espresso (8 ounces)
1 cup heavy cream
2 egg whites

Beat the yolks and the sugar in the top of a double boiler over gently simmering water until it reaches a thick and creamy consistency. Add the almond extract and the espresso. Cook, stirring constantly for 5 minutes or until mixture is thick. Remove from heat, allowing to cool completely. Meanwhile, beat the cream until it forms soft peaks. Beat the egg whites until stiff peaks form. Very gently fold half the cream and half the whites into the coffee mixture. Repeat the process with the other half. Process in an ice cream maker until frozen, or place in freezer. Dust each serving with cocoa powder.

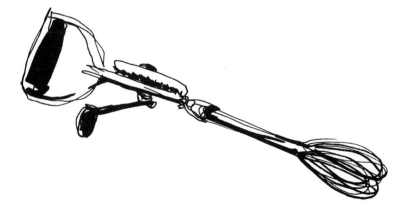

## MOCHA TRUFFLES

*Makes 36*

1 cup heavy whipping cream
2 strips lemon zest (colored part of peel)
8 ounces finely chopped bittersweet chocolate
2 tablespoons freshly brewed espresso
4 ounces butter (1 stick), at room temperature
1/4 cup unsweetened cocoa powder
1 tablespoon finely ground espresso coffee

Place cream and lemon zest in a double boiler over vigorously simmering water. Heat mixture just to simmering point. Remove lemon and discard. Add chopped chocolate. Add espresso, blend well. Cool. Beat in butter until creamy. Refrigerate until firm enough to work with; about 2 hours. Blend ground espresso and cocoa thoroughly. Shape the chocolate mixture into 1 inch balls; roll in the cocoa mixture. Refrigerate. Prior to serving, allow to stand for 10 minutes at room temperature.

NOTE: Mixture will become sticky as it warms to room temperature. Place in freezer for a few minutes to maintain a more desirable consistency if it becomes too warm while shaping.

# A SOUFFLÉ

## MOCHA SOUFFLÉ

*Serves 4*

6 ounces of semisweet chocolate
8 ounces of freshly brewed espresso
4 egg whites, at room temperature
3/4 cup vanilla sugar (see page 133)
Unsalted butter to grease soufflé dish

Preheat oven to 375°F. Butter a 6 inch soufflé dish or 4 individual soufflé dishes. Melt chocolate in a double boiler; add espresso; stir well. Set aside. Whip egg whites until soft peaks form, then gradually add sugar to the whites. Gently fold the egg white mixture into the espresso-chocolate mixture. Pour into the soufflé dish(es). Place dish(es) in a baking pan containing 2 inches of water. Bake for 35 to 40 minutes.

*Tips for Perfect Soufflés*

Folding is a gentle art, as delicate as good diplomacy. It is preferable to have some unblended spots than to overdo the process, which will mean the soufflé will not rise.

The soufflé dish you bake in must have straight sides. It is a good idea to put a "collar" around the top. Foil is easiest to work with. Tie a string around the collar to keep it from sliding. You should grease the collar as well as the dish to keep your soufflé from sticking.

# *Sources*

SPECIALTY COFFEE ROASTERS ARE SOME OF THE NICEST people that you will ever meet. They impress you as a group of people that absolutely *love* their work. More like friends than competitors, all are bound by a common love of coffee and a common pride taken in their work. Their attitudes are refreshing in a world of industries that seem to place more and more emphasis on the bottom line rather than the quality of the goods they produce.

## *SHOPPING BY MAIL OR PHONE*

Try to find your coffee and accessories locally. If you cannot, the following guide can help you find the freshest beans, the best machines and the finest accessories. An attempt was made to list roasters in different regions of the nation. This is by no means a comprehensive list of roasters or of the goods that they offer. Some roasters have less written about them than others – a fact that has no bearing on their quality. Others have been singled out for their emphasis on espresso. Your comments about these or other roasters deserving mention would be welcomed and appreciated.

Minimum orders (if any) are given, followed by credit cards accepted. MC for Mastercard, V for Visa, AMEX for American Express, and DISC for Discover. How and when the product is shipped is followed by some of the other items offered by the roasters. The information is correct to the best of my knowledge and is provided for your convenience and enjoyment.

The regions and their roasters are listed alphabetically, followed by entries for Alaska, Hawaii and Canada.

# COFFEE ROASTING COMPANIES

## EAST _____

**The Coffee Connection**              **(800) 284-JAVA**
**119 Braintree Street**               **(617) 254-1459**
**Boston, MA 02134**

Well known and respected roaster offering a wide variety of coffees and accessories. One of the most informative catalogues I have seen. A member of the *Boston Magazine* "Best of Boston" Hall of Fame. They offer a very good espresso.

*One pound minimum • MC/V/AMEX • UPS • shipped within 24 hours of roasting (twice weekly) • espresso machine • grinders • organic coffee • chocolate • catalogue and newsletter • tea*

**Dallis Bros. Inc.**
**100-30 Atlantic Avenue**
**Ozone Park, NY 11416**

**(800) 424-4252**
**(718) 845-3010**

The opening of a retail outlet marks the latest addition to the Dallis Bros. coffee tradition that dates from 1913.

*No minimum • MC/V/DISC • UPS • shipped same or next day • espresso machines • grinders • price sheet • tea*


**Gillies Coffee Company**
**160 Bleecker Street**
**New York, NY 10012**

**(718) 499-7766**

A treasure of New York's coffee culture, Gillies has been preparing its fancy espressos since Clippership days. Easy-to-understand descriptive labeling (Dark, Darker, Darkest) and fresh-as-can-be quality are a hallmark here where many of the city's best known chef-restauranteurs come for their coffee requisites. "Gillies stands as a reminder that there has always been, in the American trade, a tradition of uncompromised craftsmanship and fair value," – *Tea & Coffee Trade Journal*, 2/90. Chosen among "America's Best" by Chefs in America. Gillies was founded by Wright Gillies in 1840.

*One pound minimum • MC/V/AMEX on orders over $15 • UPS • shipped same or next day - free shipping within lower 48 • multiple espressos • catalogue and brochures • tea*

**Green Mountain Coffee Roasters**			**(800) 223-6768**
33 Coffee Lane					**(802) 244-5621**
Waterbury, VT 05676

The popularity of this New England roaster is a direct result of the enthusiasm and dedication of the owner to providing his customers with quality coffee. In addition to their coffees, Green Mountain Coffee Roasters offer their own line of environmentally safe coffee filters.

*No minimum • MC/V/AMEX • UPS • shipped same or next day - free shipping within lower 48 • grinders • catalogue • tea*


**McNulty's Tea & Coffee Company**		**(800) 356-5200**
109 Christopher Street
New York, NY 10014

*No minimum • MC/V/AMEX • UPS • shipped same or next day • organic coffee • brochure • tea*


**Nicholas Coffee Co.**				**(412) 261-4225**
23 Market Square
Pittsburgh, PA 15222

*No minimum • MC/V • UPS • shipped 2 to 3 days after order • flavorings • brochure • tea*


**Old City Coffee, Inc.**				**(215) 592-1897**
221 Church Street
Philadelphia, PA 19106

*One pound minimum • MC/V • UPS • shipped same or next day • custom blending and roasting • brochure • tea*

## Oren's Daily Roast                    (212) 779-1241
## 434 3rd Avenue
## New York, NY 10016

Being a small batch roaster (5 to 7 pounds) ensures freshness in a wide variety of coffees.

*Two pound minimum (1/2 pound per item) • MC/V/AMEX on orders over $25 • UPS • shipped same or next day • espresso machines • grinders • home roasting machine • brochure • tea*


## Porto Rico Importing Co.              (212) 477-5421
## 201 Bleecker Street
## New York, NY 10012

Very friendly and knowledgeable New York roaster featuring a different coffee on sale each week. They hold two large sales each year: a spring sale in April and Peter's birthday sale in the fall (October 22nd).

*No minimum • MC/V/AMEX/DISC • UPS • shipped same or next day • multiple espresso roasts • Torani syrups • organic coffee • espresso machines • grinders • catalogue and brochure • tea*


## M.E. Swing Company, Inc.             (202) 628-7601
## 437 11th Street NW
## Washington, DC 20004

Woodrow Wilson was president when M.E. Swing first opened their doors for business.

*No minimum • no credit cards • UPS • shipped same or next day • espresso machines • grinders • flavorings • price sheet • tea*

# MIDWEST

**Boston Stoker, Inc.**
23 North Main
Englewood, OH 45322

**(800) 827-JAVA**
**(513) 448-6528**

The owner's love of coffee and dedication to quality is evident after only a few short minutes of conversation. Boston Stoker dark roasts a variety of straight coffees that are ideal for exploring the world of straight coffee espresso.

*No minimum • MC/V • UPS • shipped same or next day • espresso machines • grinders • multiple espressos • spices • flyer • price sheet • tea*

**The Coffee Beanery**
G-3429 Pierson Place
Flushing, MI 48433

**(800) 728-2326**
**(313) 733-1020**

As of this printing the very popular Coffee Beanery has 65 stores in fourteen states. That number will have changed by the time you read this. Call the 800 number listed above for the location of the store nearest you.

*No minimum • MC/V/AMEX • UPS • shipped same or next day • espresso machines • grinders • catalogue and price sheet • tea*

## Firehouse Coffee Roasters
## 11852 Dorsett Road
## Maryland Heights, MO 63043

**(314) 298-0166**

The high percentage of Europeans in St. Louis make the darker roasts very important to the business of this roaster.

*Two and one half pound minimum • no credit cards • UPS • shipped same or next day • espresso machines • grinders • organic coffee • spices • tea*


## Gloria Jean's Coffee Bean
## 1001 Asbury Drive
## Buffalo Grove, Il 60089

**(800) 235-0555**

Gloria Jean's is a rapidly growing gourmet coffee company with over 100 independently-owned franchises nationwide. In addition to their coffees, they carry china and other gift items. Mail orders are accepted at each franchise. Call the number listed above for the location of the store nearest you.

*No minimum • MC/V/AMEX • UPS • shipped same or next day • espresso machines • grinders • tea*


## Victor Allen's Coffee & Tea
## 713 Post Road
## Madison, WI 53713

**(608) 274-4666**

A very good Wisconsin roaster and retailer providing coffees to many restaurants and retail shops throughout the region.

*No minimum • MC/V/AMEX • UPS • shipped same or next day • espresso machines • grinders • brochure • tea*

# NORTHWEST

**Batdorf & Bronson**
**513 South Capitol Way**
**Olympia, WA 98501**

**(800) 955-JAVA**
**(206) 786-6717**

An Olympia favorite and a roaster contributing to the Northwest's coffee culture.

*One half pound minimum • MC/V • UPS • shipped same or next day • organic coffee • Torani syrups • brochure • tea*

**Boyd Coffee Company**
**19730 NE Sandy Boulevard**
**Portland, OR 97230**

**(503) 666-4545**

A very well known name in Northwest coffee, Boyd offers a number of interesting food items and other accessories in addition to their coffees.

*No minimum • MC/V/AMEX • UPS • shipped same or next day • espresso machines • grinders • multiple espressos • Torani syrups • spices • brochure • tea*

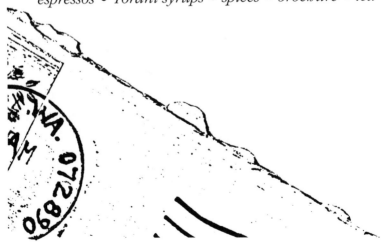

**Capt. Beans**        **(800) 423-2385**
**1825 SE Franklin**
**Unit B**
**Portland, OR 97202**

A popular Portland roaster who has a large following of area espresso bar and cart operators.

*One pound minimum • MC/V/DISC • UPS • shipped same or next day • multiple espressos*


**Caravali Coffees**        **(800) 942-JAVA**
**1301 1st Avenue**
**Seattle, WA 98101**

A well-known Seattle roaster popular with specialty shop operators, who will supply you directly with coffee or let you know where their nearest retailer is located.

*No minimum • MC/V/AMEX • UPS • shipped same or next day • grinders • organic coffee • brochure • tea*


**Coffee Corner**        **(800) 782-3414**
**591 High Street #2**        **(503) 343-7235**
**Eugene, OR 97401**

Coffee Corner espresso is a very good example of the variety to be found in espresso blends. Their espresso is smooth and without the bite that is often found in darker espressos.

*Two pound minimum • MC/V • UPS • shipped same or next day • organic coffee • brochure and price list • tea*

## Millstone Coffee Inc.          (800) 466-0300
## 729 100th Street SE
## Everett, WA 98208

Millstone coffees are found in over 4000 supermarkets in 48 states and should therefore be congratulated for making gourmet coffees so very accessible to the consumer. Millstone is the number one selling supermarket whole bean coffee in the United States.

*Five pound minimum • no credit cards • UPS • shipped same or next day • multiple espressos • price sheet*

## SBC Coffee          (800) 962-9659
## 1333 Stewart Street
## Seattle, WA 98109

Formerly named Stewart Brothers Coffee, SBC stands for "Seattle's Best Coffee." One of the oldest and most popular specialty coffee roasters in Seattle.

*One pound minimum • MC/V • shipped same or next day • multiple espressos • brochure*

**Starbucks Coffee Company**
**2203 Airport Way South**
**Seattle, WA 98134**

**(800) 445-3428**
**(206) 447-4120**

As one of the first specialty roasters in Seattle, Starbucks is largely responsible for the proliferation of the Northwest's superlative coffee culture. In addition to other local outlets, they operate 10 stores in one square mile of downtown Seattle. Starbucks has retail outlets in Washington, California, Oregon, Illinois, Colorado, and British Columbia with other locations to follow. They are to be commended for the extent and quality of their informative and educational literature and more importantly for being the largest West Coast contributor to C.A.R.E.

*Two pound minimum • MC/V/AMEX • UPS • shipped same or next day • espresso machines • grinders • catalogue and brochures*

**Torrefazione Italia, Inc.**
**320 Occidental Avenue South**
**Seattle, WA 98104**

**(800) 827-2333**
**(206) 624-5773**

Torrefazione Italia is a wonderful roaster with an emphasis on espresso. They offer seven different blends and their espressos are among the most popular with espresso bar and cart operators. A roaster true to their Italian heritage and traditions.

*One pound minimum • MC/V/AMEX • UPS • shipped within 48 hours of order • multiple espressos • brochure*

**Veneto's Coffee Company**  (206) 451-8323
**10116 NE 8th, Suite F**
**Bellevue, WA 98004**

Veneto's is a name that I heard many times (with favorable mention) around the country when I was doing research for this book. Their reputation is well deserved and their understanding of espresso is certainly reflected in their product.

*One pound minimum • MC/V • UPS • shipped within 24 hours of roasting (three times weekly) • multiple espressos • brochure*

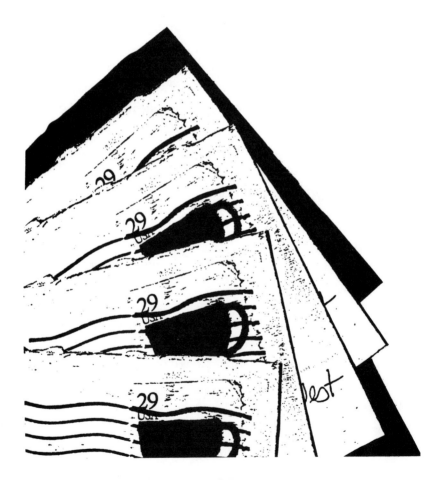

# SOUTH _____

**Broad Street Coffee Roasters**     **(919) 933-9463**
**P.O. Box 333**
**Chapel Hill, NC 27514**

The owner of this Carolina roastery is a very gracious and knowledgeable gentleman with a genuine pride in his product.

*No minimum • MC/V • UPS • shipped same or next day • espresso machines • grinders • price list • tea*


**Coffee Plantation, Ltd.**     **(800) 252-8211**
**4920 Roswell Road**     **(404) 252-4686**
**Atlanta, GA 30342**

An excellent roaster regularly selected as "Best of Atlanta" by *Atlanta Magazine*.

*No minimum • MC/V/AMEX • UPS • shipped same or next day • espresso machines • grinders • spices • brochure • tea*


**The Fine Grind**     **(901) 685-0408**
**4465 Poplar Avenue #102**
**Memphis, TN 38117**
     **Indianapolis (317) 635-2924**

Separate roasters of similar character individually owned by two sisters.

*No minimum • AMEX • UPS • shipped same or next day • espresso machines • grinders • home roasting machine • flavorings • brochure • tea*

**House of Coffee Beans, Inc.**　　　　**(800) 422-1799**
2520 Rice Boulevard　　　　　　　　　**(713) 524-0057**
Houston, TX 77005

One of the oldest roasters in the great State of Texas.

*No minimum • MC/V • UPS • shipped same or next day
• espresso machines • grinders • organic coffee • price
sheet • tea*


**La Crèmé's Coffee & Tea**　　　　**(214) 369-4188**
4448 Lovers Lane
Dallas, TX 75225

A fine Dallas roaster supplying coffee to almost half of the
top 100 restaurants in Dallas (restaurant list compiled by
*D Magazine*).

*One pound minimum • MC/V/AMEX • UPS • shipped
same or next day • Gaggia service center • brochure • tea*


**J. Martinez & Company**　　　　**(800) 642-5282**
3230-A Peachtree Road NE　　　　**(404) 233-4196**
Atlanta, GA 30305

In addition to their Don Giovanni Espresso Bellissimo, this
very knowledgeable and respected roaster offers a variety
of single estate coffees. One of the most famous is the
lovingly grown and impeccably processed La Minita
Tarrazu from Costa Rica.

*No minimum • MC/V/AMEX/DISC • UPS • shipped
same or next day • exotic condiments • catalogue •
tea*

## The Coffee Plantation, Inc.
## 680 South Mill Avenue #101
## Tempe, AZ 85281

**(602) 829-7878**

The Coffee Plantation is proof that the popularity of quality espresso is not confined to cooler climates.

*One pound minimum • MC/V • UPS • shipped same or next day • multiple espressos • espresso machines • grinders • Torani syrups • brochure and price sheet • tea*

## Village Roaster
## 9255 W. Alameda Avenue
## Lakewood, Co 80226

**(800) 237-3822**
**(303) 238-8718**

The Village Roaster puts out a newsletter called The Daily Grind that provides you with informative and entertaining information about coffee.

*No minimum • MC/V • UPS • shipped same or next day • spices • brochure • tea*

## White Cloud Mountain Coffee
## P.O. Box 1737
## Boise, ID 83701

**(800) 627-0309**

*No minimum • MC/V • UPS • shipped same or next day • grinders • Torani syrups • catalogue • tea*

# WEST COAST _____

## Caffè Roma                                    (415) 296-7662
## 526 Columbus Avenue
## San Francisco, CA 94133

A roaster who specializes in espresso and is always work-ing to achieve the correct balance of roast and blend.

*Two pound minimum • MC/V • UPS • Shipped same or next day • biscotti • multiple espressos*


## Capricorn Coffees      Nationwide  (800) 541-0758
## 353 Tenth Street       California   (800) 543-8388
## San Francisco, CA 94103             (415) 621-8500

*One pound minimum • MC/V • UPS • shipped same or next day • espresso machines • grinders • custom blending • organic coffee • brochure • tea*


## The Coffee Critic                            (415) 342-8558
## 106 South El Casino Real
## San Mateo, CA 94401

Great espresso begins with great green coffee. The Coffee Critic's green coffee broker is M.P. Mountanos, a broker with four generations of experience in fine coffees.

*Two pound minimum • no credit cards • UPS • shipped same or next day • multiple espressos • espresso machines • grinders • Torani syrups • brochure and price list • tea*

**Coffee Emporium**                        **(213) 823-4446**
4325 Glencoe Avenue
Marina Del Rey, CA 90292

*Ten dollar minimum • MC/V/AMEX • UPS • shipped same or next day • price sheet • tea*

**Diedrich Coffee**                        **(714) 646-0432**
474 E. 17th Street, Suite 205
Costa Mesa, CA 92627

The Diedrich name is very well known and respected in the world of specialty coffee.

*One pound minimum • MC/V • UPS • shipped same or next day • brochure • tea*

**Kelly's Coffee Factory**                 **(714) 727-3764**
15251 Barranca Parkway
Irvine, CA 92718

Kelly's has 20 locations west of the Mississippi and are in the process of planning another 5 stores.

*One pound minimum • MC/V/AMEX • UPS • shipped same or next day • espresso machines • price sheet • tea*

**Los Gatos Coffee Roasting Company**      **(800) 877-7718**
101 West Main Street                       **(408) 354-3263**
Los Gatos, CA 95030

You need only pay the difference between regular ground and next day delivery if you would like your coffee shipped to you using next day service.

*Two pound minimum • MC/V • UPS • shipped same or next day - free shipping within lower 48 • espresso machines • grinders • Torani syrups • brochure • tea*

**Mr. Espresso**　　　　　　　　　　　　　**(415) 835-3944**
**696 3rd Street**
**Oakland, CA 94607**

Mr. Espresso roasts their blends over an oak-wood fire.

*Ten pound minimum • no credit cards • brochure*


**J.R. Muggs   California**　　　　　　　**(800) 540-6847**
**1801 Larkspur Landing**　　　　　　　**(415) 925-9228**
**Larkspur, CA 94939**

J.R. Muggs' walls are home to over 5000 coffee mugs.

*Two pound minimum • MC/V • UPS • shipped same or next day • organic coffee • brochure • tea*


**Pannikin Coffee & Tea**　　　　　　　**(800) 232-6482**
**1205 J Street**　　　　　　　　　　　**(619) 239-1257**
**San Diego, CA 92101**

Pannikin has been providing quality coffee to the San Diego area since they opened their first store in 1968.

*No minimum • MC/V/AMEX • UPS • shipped same or next day • price sheet and Christmas catalogue   • tea*


**Peet's Coffee & Tea**　　　　　　　　**(800) 999-2132**
**P.O. Box 8247**
**Emeryville, CA 94662**

Peet's is one of the largest and most respected roasters in the San Francisco Bay Area. Their longstanding commitment to quality continues to serve as an inspiration to many in the specialty coffee business.

*Two pound minimum • MC/V • UPS • shipped same or next day • spices • price sheet • tea*

**Polly's Gourmet Coffee**                    **(213) 433-2996.**
**4606 Second Street**
**Long Beach, CA 90803**

*No minimum • MC/V • UPS • shipped same or next day • espresso machines • grinders • custom blending and roasting • brochure and newsletter • tea*

**See's Coffee**                    **(805) 498-6111**
**PO Box 515**
**Newbury Park, CA 91319-0515**

Just prior to the printing of this book, See's indicated that they planned to begin accepting some charge cards in the near future.

*Two pound minimum • no credit cards • UPS • shipped same or next day • price sheet*

**Thanksgiving Coffee Company**                    **(800) 648-6491**
**P.O. Box 1918**
**Fort Bragg, CA 95437**

The owners of Thanksgiving Coffee are committed to improving the lives of the people in the coffee producing countries. They offer an impressive selection of organic coffees and a catalogue that is both very attractive and informative.

*No minimum • MC/V/AMEX • UPS • shipped same or next day • grinders • organic coffee • catalogue • tea*

# ALASKA ─────────────────────

### Cafe Del Mundo
### 229 East 51st Avenue
### Anchorage, AK 99503

### (907) 562-2326

The largest roaster in the very large state of Alaska.

*Twelve dollar minimum • MC/V/AMEX • US Mail or FED EX • shipped same or next day • espresso machines • grinders • organic coffee • Torani syrups • spices • price sheet • tea*


### Heritage Coffee
### 625 West Seventh Sreet
### Juneau, AK 99801

### Alaska

### (907) 780-4282
### (800) 478-JAVA

A very popular coffee calendar with pictures from the world of coffee is available from Heritage Coffee Productions. For more information, call (907) 586-1114.

*Two pound minimum • MC/V/AMEX • US Mail • shipped same or next day • espresso machines • grinders • organic coffee • Torani syrups • price sheet • tea*


### Kaladi Brothers Coffee Company
### 6921 Brayton Drive, Suite A
### Anchorage, AK 99507

### (907) 344-5483

A very knowledgeable Alaskan roaster whose majority of business is espresso. They offer an instructional espresso book for owners and operators of commercial machines.

*Two pound minimum • MC/V • US Mail • shipped same or next day • upper-end espresso machines • grinders • Torani syrups • Ghiradelli Cocoa • brochure • tea*

# HAWAII

**Lion Coffee**
**894 Queen Street**
**Honolulu, HI 96813**

**(800) 338-8353**
**(808) 521-3479**

It may be the Island life, the coffee, or a combination of the two that makes the people at Lion so cheerful and so helpful. Regardless of the reason, you will enjoy their friendly enthusiasm.

*Two 10 ounce bags • MC/V • FED EX • shipped same or next day • catalogue • newsletter*

# CANADA

**The Second Cup**
**3300 Bloor Street West**
**Suite 2900**
**Box 54**
**Etobicoke, ON M8X 2X3 CANADA**

**(416) 236-0053**

Good coffee in Canada is closer than you think. The Second Cup Coffee Company was established in 1975, has over 170 stores across Canada and is still growing. Although they do not offer a mail order service, they will be happy to provide you with the location of the store nearest you. Their size belies the warm, personable service you can expect from the people of The Second Cup.

Please address all inquiries and comments to:

**Nick Jurich**

Missing Link Press, Inc.

3213 West Wheeler Street

Suite 179

Seattle, WA 98199

# INDEX